9

Pelléas &
Mélisande
Debussy

The last scene of Act Four designed by Jussaume for the first production, Paris, 1902. (Le Théàtre, Stuart-Liff Collection)

Preface

This series, published under the auspices of English National Opera and The Royal Opera, aims to prepare audiences to enjoy and evaluate opera performances. Each book contains the complete text, set out in the original language together with a current performing translation. The accompanying essays have been commissioned as general introductions to aspects of interest in each work. As many illustrations and musical examples as possible have been included because the sound and spectacle of opera are clearly central to any sympathetic appreciation of it. We hope that, as ideal companions to the opera should be, they are well-informed, witty and attractive.

Nicholas John
Series Editor

Pelléas & Mélisande

Claude Debussy

Opera Guide Series Editor: Nicholas John

Published in association with English National Opera and The Royal Opera

John Calder · London
Riverrun Press · New York

First published in Great Britain, 1982, by
John Calder (Publishers) Ltd., 18 Brewer Street,
London W1R 4AS

and

First published in the U.S.A., 1982, by
Riverrun Press Inc.,
175 Fifth Avenue,
New York, NY 10010

BRITISH LIBRARY CATALOGUING DATA
Debussy, Claude
    Pelléas et Mélisande — (English National Opera guide; 9)
    1. Debussy, Claude. Pelléas et Mélisande
    2. Operas — Librettos
    I. Title   II. Maeterlinck, Maurice
    III. John, Nicholas   IV. Series
    782.1'092'4   ML 410.D28
ISBN 0 7145 3906 6

SUBSIDISED BY THE
Arts Council
OF GREAT BRITAIN

John Calder (Publishers) Ltd, English National Opera and The
Royal Opera House, Covent Garden Ltd receive financial assis-
tance from the Arts Council of Great Britain. English National
Opera also receives financial assistance from the Greater London
Council.

Typeset in Plantin by Margaret Spooner Typesetting
Printed and bound in Great Britain by Collins, Glasgow.

Contents

List of Illustrations

Something Borrowed, Something New.

Hugh Macdonald

Debussy is universally recognised as one of the most original voices in twentieth-century music, the well from which countless later composers have drawn. Ravel, Messiaen and Boulez, for all their individuality, seem members of a Debussy dynasty in the way that Cavalli was the child of Monteverdi or Rameau of Lully. His originality is not in question: that tiny fragment, the *Prélude à l'après-midi d'un faune*, of 1893, alone proclaims a new musical cosmos. Yet Debussy's deep and complex musical roots are at least partly visible in nearly everything he wrote. To examine them is to look at a panorama of European music in the later nineteenth century, and to survey the cultural milieu in which the ardent young composer grew up.

Not that Debussy was uncritically receptive to everything he heard. He was severe on Beethoven and Schumann and described Berlioz as 'not a musician at all'. But he absorbed the newer currents in French music and the tremendous urge towards regeneration prompted by the humiliations of the Franco-Prussian war. Gounod and Thomas had already moulded a characteristically lyrical style of opera whose strengths were melodiousness and the lighter emotions cast aside by the grand opera traditions of Meyerbeer and Verdi, as well as balletic and scenic enchantment. Massenet inherited this mantle, and his craftsmanship and stylishness made him the most successful composer of opera in Paris at a time when Debussy, who was perfectly happy to lean towards Massenet in his early works, was anxious to prove his own expertise in the theatre. Ultimately, of course, *Pelléas et Mélisande* avoided the pitfalls that Massenet's example might have put in Debussy's way, but the shared background is constantly evident. Many fragments in the orchestral part recall Massenet's shapely manner and, for a moment, the vocal line also in the Act Four love duet, the first music of the opera to be written.

From Saint-Saens Debussy learned to admire French classical music and to uphold national values, providing common ground in later years when Debussy's touchiness and Saint-Saens's bitterness made mutual admiration impossible. In Lalo Debussy admired the delicate orchestration of the ballet *Namouna* (part of which was actually done by Gounod when Lalo fell ill). The tradition of invoking the orient was almost an obsession in French music ever since Félicien David's runaway hit *Le désert* in 1844, followed by Gounod's *The Queen of Sheba*, Bizet's *Pearl Fishers*, Massenet's *The King of Lahore*, Delibes's *Lakmé* and innumerable others. *Lakmé* Debussy actually derided as 'sham, imitative Oriental bric-à-brac', but he knew full well the appeal and the acceptability of chinoiserie when he composed his *Pagodes*, just as he knew he was joining the queue of French purveyors of Spanish colour when he composed *La puerta del vino*.

These exotic odours are undetectable in *Pelléas et Mélisande*, frequent though they are elsewhere in Debussy's work. There is a more pertinent kinship with the music of Fauré, whose freely modal inflexions surely influenced Debussy's departure from rigid tonal movement more than is usually credited. As song-writers Fauré and Debussy had much in common: a taste for Verlaine, a refined sense of vocal melody, a fondness for flowing inner parts in a water-like texture, and much else; Fauré (with Debussy's knowledge) provided music for a London production of *Pelléas et Mélisande* in 1898. In Debussy's opera one hears Fauré in the music's constant avoidance of hard diatonic cadences and in the restless orchestral figures in Golaud's scene with Yniold. One other French composer,

Mary Garden as Mélisande. She created the role and sang it in many countries. She gave the first performance in America and Frances Alda remembered: 'She was so still. Just that one little phrase: 'Il fait froid ici', as it came from her lips, and you shivered under the chill winds that blew between the worlds of the real and the unreal. Contrasted with it, (Lucrezia) Bori's rendering of the line sounded like a schoolgirl who steps out of bed without her slippers'. (Royal College of Music)

Satie, must be accorded his due here since he appears to have led the way when Debussy was himself, at the Conservatoire, tentatively exploring advanced chords of ninths and elevenths. Satie delighted in them in a playful spirit of irreverence never channelled into the higher reaches of art, whereas Debussy gradually emancipated these discords from their functional purposes, and used their sonorous qualities as expressive and evocative in their own right. By the time *Pelléas et Mélisande* was composed he had perfected a harmonic language in which advanced chords move freely with or without a functional, progressive role. The issue of parallel fifths and octaves, so hotly contested between Debussy and his mentors since they are forbidden in classical harmonic practice, is simply no issue at all: chords move in parallel, conjunct or disjunct motion at will. Edward Lockspeiser also sees Satie's influence in the characterisation of Yniold, even in the innocence of Pelléas and Mélisande themselves.

So for all Debussy's debts to his French inheritance he had largely outgrown the shallower mannerisms of his elders by 1893, when *Pelléas et Mélisande* was begun. Lyricism remains to a certain extent and expressiveness in abundance, but for word-setting and many elements of the orchestral part Debussy had been looking further afield. The most significant contribution was undoubtedly Mussorgsky's *Boris Godunov*. Debussy was reported not to have shown much interest in this work when lent a score in 1889, but *Pelléas et Mélisande* suggests strongly either that he took more interest than he admitted or that he had absorbed prevalent ideas on vocal writing during his Russian visits in 1881 and 1882. For *Boris Godunov* is not the only work to exhibit realist tendencies, simply the most powerful. Mussorgsky was applying artistic principles which had been worked out by literary critics and transferred to music with some success by Dargomyzhsky in his very dramatic songs, and later, with singlemindedness bordering on obsession, in his opera *The Stone Guest*. Imperial censorship, it was argued, laid upon the artist the obligation to portray real life as vividly as he could since social reformers were prevented from doing so. Only as fiction could the iniquities of the tsarist system be attacked. Fancy artistic language and imaginative fictions were thus discredited and the follies and injustices of real life portrayed in vivid detail. In Tolstoy's minutely circumstantial map of human relations or in Mussorgsky's brilliantly direct songs, the Russian genius cut through centuries of carefully constructed artistic formulae: after an experimental unfinished setting of Gogol's *The Marriage* in 1868 in which themes, motifs and lyrical writing were scrupulously avoided, he went on to set Pushkin's *Boris Godunov*, making some compromises with inherited opera but sweeping aside the heroic values of *bel canto* in vocal writing of supreme naturalness and force, accompanied by spontaneous orchestral gestures which also belie the patterns of traditional operatic technique. *Boris* remained an unchallenged masterpiece while Tchaikovsky and Rimsky-Korsakov (with the single exception of *Mozart and Salieri* of 1892) composed thoroughly operatic operas without demur. Only Debussy, Janáček and Bartók pursued the ideal of realistic word-setting with any conviction or success.

In the case of *Pelléas et Mélisande* this implies that the vocal writing shows none of the declamatory excesses of Italian grand opera nor even the lyrical shapeliness of Gounod, Bizet and Massenet. Instead, he treats the words much more nearly as plain speech, and since Maeterlinck had written them as a play which Debussy now wished to respect for its theatrical quality, the lines are delivered with very little 'singing' implied. The emphasis is on stress and phrase patterns, on clarity of diction (the words are never drowned by the orchestra) and on a naturalness aided by the complete lack of motivic or thematic shape in the vocal writing. This is felt all the more strongly when, exceptionally, the characters utter lines of actual melody; as for example Pelléas's '*Je venais du côté de la mer*' in Act One, Scene Three, or Mélisande's '*Fermez les yeux et tâchez de dormir*' in Act Two, Scene Two. Mélisande's song as she combs her hair at the window in Act Three, Scene One, makes a striking contrast with the real drama of which she is unknowingly a part since her utterances are otherwise impulsive, shaped by the rise and fall of syllables, not by musical logic.

Jean Perrier, who created the role of Pelléas, Paris 1902 (Stuart-Liff Collection)

Hector Dufranne, who created the role of Golaud, Paris 1902. (Stuart-Liff Collection)

Along with *Boris Godunov* the strongest formative influence on *Pelléas et Mélisande* was Wagner, or more particularly *Parsifal*. The complex history of Wagner's influence in France has been expounded by many writers, and the question of *Parsifal's* paternity of *Pelléas et Mélisande* thoroughly and skillfully explored by Robin Holloway in his book *Debussy and Wagner* (London, 1979). Debussy himself experienced the contradictory thrusts of admiration and rejection and thus always spoke of Wagner with some caution, knowing both his debt and his eagerness to outgrow it. In the matter of vocal writing one can easily observe that *Pelléas et Mélisande* does not call for Wagnerian voices, but much more nearly singing actors; on the other hand the predominant musical action resides in the orchestra, as it does in Wagner, where the motifs are presented, discussed and interwoven in an acceptably Wagnerian manner (not that Berlioz and Verdi had not been doing much the same all along). The orchestra in *Pelléas et Mélisande* is handled with far more restraint than Wagner ever showed, even in *Parsifal*, and comes forward prominently only in the interludes mainly composed at a later stage to facilitate scene changes. But the harmonic colour is often undeniably Wagnerian, for all the shifting triads and extended chords which Wagner had never ventured upon.

We would be more aware of Debussy's musical independence from Wagner if Maeterlinck himself had not deliberately set out to evoke the remote legendary world of kings and princesses, forests and castles, conforming to Wagnerian orthodoxy of the 1880s. As has often been pointed out, the theme of jealousy and of a stolen bride closely resembles that of *Tristan und Isolde*. The action is timeless and the symbolism prominent. A taste for decaying castles and sinister action of no clear significance came in any case to French writers from Edgar Allan Poe, adored by Baudelaire, Mallarmé, Maeterlinck, Debussy and many others. In Poe they found a prophet of their faith in allusion and symbolism, whose strength lay in the very opposite of the Russians' realism. In the Symbolist aesthetic, words no longer referred merely to objects and actions. They were deliberately used, instead, to evoke musical as well as linguistic response and to call up the shadows behind literal meaning. Alliterated consonants, obscure fantastic words, ornate syntax and suggestive poetic conceits widened artistic horizons by transferring colours to music as Skryabin did in *Prometheus*, or tastes to music, as Huysmans in *A Rebours*, and, in particular, by deepening the musical content of poetry and the poetic content of music. In Wagner, with his contrived archaic language and alliterative verse, his devotion to legend and to potent symbols such as swords, spears, ravens, swans, rainbows, potions and all the apparatus of the music drama, and in his conviction that musician, poet and dramatist in his own person became one, they found the basis of an artistic faith that conquered France and spawned Wagnerian poems, dramas, symphonies, even novels, in profusion.

In *Pelléas et Mélisande* Maeterlinck's play and Debussy's music fell to some extent outside the expected norms of the movement. Maeterlinck, it is true, filled his play with symbols, often to the point of naïveté – animals of many kinds, gates, the tower, hair, water, the clock, and especially blindness – but he deliberately avoided fanciful language and wrote in the plainest prose. The contrast between the apparent clarity of every utterance and its unfathomable meaning is thus emphasised to brilliant effect, and the horrifying immediacy of the drama is greatly strengthened. For Debussy this simple language was ideal since opera can never do justice to poetic elaboration anyway and since he particularly strove for understatement as an escape from Wagnerian hyperbole and as a potent dramatic device. As for the symbolism, he again avoided the methodical application of motifs to ideas and images. There is, for example, no motif for blindness. He made no attempt to underline references forward or back and used a much more straightforward scheme of motifs which embrace the principal characters and a few abstractions such as 'the declaration of love' (Maurice Emmanuel tentatively identified thirteen motifs and Roger Nichols here suggests forty examples), all loose enough to subject the composer to no awkward constraints. Arkel has no motif, but his music has more muscular substance than the other characters, perhaps because he sees (despite his blindness) — or thinks he sees — how things will turn out. His radiant hopes for a new era are cruelly betrayed by events, and his personal tragedy is at least as great as that of the others. His seeing is illusory after all; he is as blind as everyone else.

Symbolism could never extend the aesthetics of music very far. Problems of setting words to music and the perennial question of poetry vying with music for the hegemony of opera had been intensively debated for at least three centuries. Debussy had no wish to add mounds of theory to the accumulated pile as Wagner had done. He simply left the heavy symbolism of Maeterlinck's drama as he found it and used music for its time-honoured purpose as generator of atmosphere, tension, colour, memory, and so on. By eschewing lyrical singing he imposed on himself a severe but powerfully effective restriction which would have consigned him to oblivion, like Dargomyzhsky, had he not drawn out of himself at the most propitious moment of his career, like Mussorgsky, a fount of invention and ideas that commands the listener's attention and admiration.

Pelléas et Mélisande was Debussy's only completed opera. Perhaps with hindsight one might conclude that he created a new type of opera and solved its problems so completely that no second opera could be imagined. Much the same is said of Beethoven's *Fidelio* from time to time. But this argument scarcely accords with the fact of Debussy's lifelong involvement with the theatre in its many forms, with opera, drama, ballet and incidental music. Certainly Debussy searched long and hard for a libretto he liked which would inspire him as successfully as Maeterlinck's did in 1893. But even *Pelléas et Mélisande* almost joined the ranks of the unfinished projects: he thought of it, in André Schaeffner's words, 'as a sort of tapestry which would unroll itself in an unknown manner with the characters hardly detaching themselves from the decor embroidered by his music'. With his passion for Poe, Debussy certainly saw *Pelléas et Mélisande* as a darker and more sinister drama than Maeterlinck did: there is no pallor in the score despite the common notion of Debussy's music as impressionist watercolour. In 1890, three years before *Pelléas et Mélisande*, he was already preoccupied with Poe's *The Fall of the House of Usher*, a darkly mysterious story to which he later returned in the last ten years of his life, completing a draft of at least the first scene. Those years before *Pelléas et Mélisande* was begun also saw projects based on Villiers de l'Isle Adam's *Axel*, and Maeterlinck's *La Princesse Maleine*. The first of these concerns the wealthy inhabitant of an isolated medieval castle enticed, in vain, by a Kundry-like Rosicrucian nun to a life of sensuous pleasure to which he is too jaded to yield; the second again concerns a mysterious prison in which a frail and terrified princess is confined. Yet another libretto which passed through Debussy's hands in 1895 (when *Pelléas et Mélisande* was already substantially complete in draft) was based on Balzac's *La grande bretèche* about a mysterious house (like that of Usher) concealing sinister secrets. Another Poe story, *The Devil in the Belfry*, preoccupied Debussy in his last years as a companion-piece to *The Fall of the House of Usher*, but despite many references to work in progress scarcely more than a fragment of music survives. It was not the success of *Pelléas et Mélisande* that foreclosed any later operatic project but a deep-seated hesitation which aborted all kinds of plans in his later years, not only operatic ones. Complex conflicts in his artistic nature arose at least in part from the interweaving of tradition and innovation, and allowed him no easy solution in terms of form and style. At a time when far-reaching new ideas were emerging in the works of Schoenberg, Skryabin and Stravinsky – to mention only the composers — certainty in artistic matters was nobody's prerogative.

Significantly enough the one opera other than *Pelléas et Mélisande* even to approach completion came before Debussy's preoccupation with dark abodes and their doomed, diseased or decaying inmates. This was a libretto by the Wagnerian Catulle Mendès, partly based on Corneille's *Le Cid*, under the title *Rodrigue et Chimène*. It was begun about 1889 and designed to be readily acceptable by the Opéra in order to further Debussy's career, although since Massenet's *Le Cid* of 1885 was an established success there, it is hard to see how librettist and composer imagined another opera on the same subject might succeed. But then Debussy was equally prepared, in 1909, to contemplate an opera on *Tristan et Iseult*, inviting an even more risky comparison. *Rodrigue et Chimène* survives in a remarkably complete state, even though not orchestrated. Like *The Fall of the House of Usher*, performed in part at Yale in 1977, it may yet come to a modern reconstruction and performance which will shed abundant light on the decisive period just before the emergence of his first masterpieces.

Taking the longer view, *Pelléas et Mélisande* reveals neither the grandeur nor the satirical tone that characterises French opera in other periods, especially not the grandeur and spectacle, since there is neither dance nor chorus (except the off-stage '*Hoé*' in Act One). It indulges in neither lyricism nor charm. But it is an intensely literary work and in that respect it satisfies the deep-seated French conviction that literary values override musical values and that the mind, in opera, should be concentrated on the text. It is certainly not a shallow work; it is replete with meaning; it is both bewildering and disturbing. But what that meaning is no critic and no listener can readily or convincingly say.

A Musical Synopsis

Roger Nichols

'My ideal is a short libretto with unhampered movement between scenes. I find the three unities irrelevant. The places and characters need to be varied from scene to scene and the characters shouldn't engage in discussions or arguments: as I see it they are controlled by life, by destiny.' Debussy voiced these thoughts some three years before coming across Maeterlinck's play in 1893. The remarkable coincidence in the aesthetic viewpoints of playwright and composer has often been remarked upon and the good fortune of the encounter is emphasised when we look at the many operatic projects Debussy later attempted and discarded.

At first hearing, Debussy's opera may seem to have little in common with those that formed the French repertory of the time and still less in common with the music-dramas of Wagner which were at last being heard in their entirety on the French stage (*Siegfried* and *Götterdämmerung*, like *Pelléas*, received their first Paris performances in 1902). But Debussy admired both Wagner and Massenet, even if somewhat guiltily, and the attentive listener to *Pelléas* will recognise here and there not only the 'ghost of old Klingsor' but the fleeting shadow of Manon. Nonetheless they *are* only ghosts and shadows, far removed from the relentlessly detailed figures of Zola's novels or, come to that, of Charpentier's *Louise*, a work Debussy heartily detested. During the nine years in which he intermittently worked on *Pelléas* Debussy was haunted by the thought of what his beloved dream might become in the all too solid flesh. In the event he was not completely disappointed, and the further material sign of his success, his promotion to Chevalier de la Légion d'honneur, at least gave pleasure to his parents. But his real success was in less material terms, in the impact his opera had on the young; not just on composers like Ravel, but on writers like Jacques Rivière, later the editor of the *Nouvelle Revue Française*: 'It is not generally appreciated what *Pelléas et Mélisande* meant for those of us between 16 and 20 who were present at its birth. It was a miraculous world, a cherished paradise where we could escape from our troubles. . . We knew the secret door and the outside world had no more hold upon us'.

Debussy set Maeterlinck's play more or less word for word, but he did cut out four scenes altogether: Act One scene one, Act Two scene four, Act Three scene one and Act Five scene one, the first and last of these being played by the castle servants. It is understandable that Debussy preferred to launch his opera with the appearance of one of the protagonists and also to follow the cataclysm at the end of Act Four with the direct result of that cataclysm. The function of Greek chorus assumed by Maeterlinck's servants is taken on most powerfully by Debussy's music: throughout the opera he continually comments on both plot and personal relationships, often by means of 'motifs of association'. As Professor Macdonald has pointed out, Debussy 'avoided the methodical application of motifs to ideas and images'. Where Wagner 'motivised' everything that moved or had its being, Debussy is more selective and we may indeed be unsure at times of what is a motif and what is not. For this reason example [17] is labelled with a question mark. As with all symbols labelling must be tentative if it is not to impose damaging limitations on the listener's response. Readers are asked to bear this in mind when reading what follows.

*

During a prologue of twenty-one bars the curtain stays down, while the orchestra depicts the forest where the first scene is set. Lower strings and bassoons intone a theme of gloom [1], leading to the theme associated with Golaud [2], its hesitant rhythm and outline reflecting his lack of inner purpose (of outward purposefulness he has more than his share, as we shall see). A more fully harmonised repeat of [1] leads to the theme [3] associated with Mélisande, here as often, entrusted to the solo oboe. The curtain rises to reveal Mélisande at the edge of a well ('*une fontaine*'). She is motionless and silent and Golaud [1] comes along the forest path without seeing her. He has been hunting but has lost both the boar he wounded and his own hounds. Suddenly he hears sobbing ([4] on the oboe is typical of Debussy's habits of deriving his ideas as much from colours and rhythms as from melodic lines, cf. [3]). He sees Mélisande and ask her why she is crying. Her only reply is to beg him not to touch her. The pattern of evasive answers is set and marked by Debussy with abrupt changes of pace, texture and rhythm. Golaud has established that she was born far from this forest and that she too is lost, when he sees something glistening at the bottom of the well [5]. It is a crown, given to Mélisande by a mysterious 'him' whose identity we never discover. Golaud, not unreasonably, offers to retrieve it, but the force of Mélisande's prohibition of any such move makes his reasonable kindness seem like base materialism. She in turn questions him as to his name, and through his answer, 'I am Prince Golaud, grandson of old Arkel King of Allemonde', the theme [6] of royalty (? Maurice Emmanuel calls it 'destiny') emerges on 'cellos and bassoons. After much anxious hesitation, expressed in the orchestra by repeated octaves off the beat, Golaud persuades her to come with him — the lost leading the lost.

The orchestral interlude takes us from the forest to a room in Arkel's castle. At least, that is its overt dramatic function, but musically it digests and assimilates [1] and [2], eventually combining them, [6] now on two trumpets assuring us that Golaud's outward confidence is secure enough. Geneviève, the mother of Golaud and Pelléas (it seems likely she bore Golaud to the elder of Arkel's sons and Pelléas to the younger),reads out to Arkel a letter Golaud has written to his half-brother, in which he says that he has been married to Mélisande for six months (where he has been in the meantime is another of the many undisclosed facts). Still he knows almost nothing about her: [7] is a good example of Debussy's understated setting of this scene, in which the vocal lines are even more closely modelled on everyday French speech than they are elsewhere in the opera. Golaud is nervous of how Arkel will receive the news, for all his kind intentions; and the rather thick bassoon and horn chord at this point looks forward to the sound of the first trombone entry when Arkel in fact gives his reply — 'no comment'. He will not fight destiny. Perhaps everything happens with some reason, he says, and the appearance of [6] in octaves on thc strings suggests that such humility may be a proper concomitant of royal status. Geneviève's worries about Golaud's future are interrupted by the arrival of Pelléas. His theme [8], though not so hesitant as Golaud's, never develops; it merely oscillates. Pelléas has been crying because of another letter, from his friend Marcellus, who thinks he is going to die and wants Pelléas to come to him. Arkel tells him to stay: Pelléas's own father is ill and who knows what Golaud's return will bring?

The brief but concentrated interlude combines themes [2] and [3] for the first time in the form [9], and the whole passage indicates that Debussy turned here to Wagner, whether consciously or not. The third scene takes place in front of the castle, where Geneviève and the newly-arrived Mélisande are in conversation. Geneviève barely has time to temper Mélisande's amazement at the sombre gardens and the forests all around before Pelléas joins them. He prophesies a storm, 'but the sea is very calm this evening' [10]: the vocal anticipation of [2] on muted horn is not just for unity's sake — Golaud too is calm 'at the moment'. A ship sails out of the port to the sound of sailors' cries (the only chorus part in the

Richard Stilwell (Pelléas), Joseph Rouleau (Arkel) and Yvonne Minton (Geneviève) at Covent Garden in 1974. (photo: Donald Southern)

opera [11]) and when the mist clears Mélisande recognises it as the one in which she arrived. The counterpoint of themes [2], [3], [11], vocal line and bass marks a high point in the opera of textural complexity, in contrast with the music that follows as darkness falls. Pelléas draws Mélisande's attention to the noise of the sea (descending triads), and as he leads her by the arm back into the castle this descending pattern fuses magically with [3], seeming to drag it down against its will [12]. The Act ends, appropriately, on a question and an unresolved dissonance [13].

A well in the park — and the sounds of flute [8], clarinet and harp set the scene. Pelléas and Mélisande enter [14] and it soon becomes clear that this outing has no conscious purpose other than innocent pleasure. Mélisande is drawn to the well which, says Pelléas, once had miraculous powers; the orchestral accompaniment [15] beautifully illustrates first the sound of water, then a sense of wonderment, in the unexpected, spreading triads. They revel in the stillness and Mélisande lies down so that she can look right to the bottom of the well. Pelléas is anxious that she might fall in [16] but is sidetracked by the sight of her long blonde hair tumbling loose. She begins to play with Golaud's ring, throwing it higher and higher above the water, enjoying the risk of losing it. From here the conversation proceeds in mosaic fashion. Mélisande's hair, Pelléas's anxiety, memories of Golaud finding her by another such well and Mélisande playing with the ring; all these topics intertwine, the 'circular' ring theme [17] taking on the menacing dotted rhythm of [2]. Inevitably, the ring drops into the water and disappears. Or

15

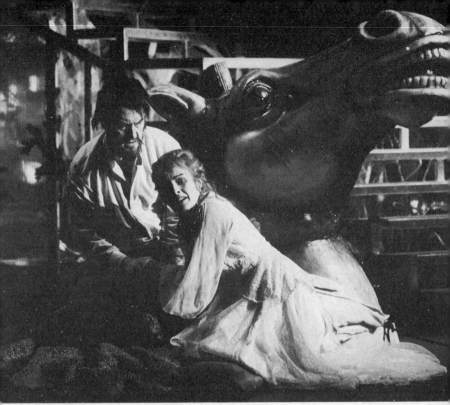

Neil Howlett (Golaud) and Eilene Hannan (Mélisande) in Harry Kupfer's 1981 ENO production. (photo: Clive Barda)

at least Mélisande is convinced it has disappeared. Pelléas, like Golaud in Act One scene one, sees it but is dissuaded from retrieving it. The pervasive circularity of [18] pictures the aimlessness to which Mélisande condemns him. Pelléas urges her to tell Golaud 'the truth': Pelléas, the innocent, has never had a moment's worry about this slippery abstraction and takes her home while the orchestra play [14], to which they both entered, at the same pitch —the whole scene is thus rendered circular, enclosed, hermetic and private, establishing an intimacy between Pelléas and Mélisande despite the innocence of the outward action.

The focus shifts during the interlude from Pelléas to Golaud, from [8] to [2], and from light to heavy orchestration. Golaud is on his bed, Mélisande at his pillow. His horse threw him suddenly at the twelfth stroke of midday (Mélisande's ring fell into the well at this precise moment: Pelléas's anxiety theme [16] makes the point). Golaud is not badly hurt, but is troubled as to why the horse should have done such a thing. Mélisande tries to minister to him, [18], but Golaud is an unresponsive patient and insists on his resilience [2]. A version of [3] on the oboe tells him and us, in advance of the text, that Mélisande is crying. She says she is *'malade ici'*; characteristically he misunderstands, ignoring *'ici'* and asking what the illness is. Debussy again uses [18], but Golaud's concern for Mélisande is not of the same stamp as hers for him, and the intervals become distorted as he begins to interrogate her. Having established that no person has done her harm, he turns to the gloomy surroundings, the dark forests, and the fact that everybody in the castle is old (not true, but Golaud does not count Pelléas worthy of consideration). Mélisande admits she would like to see the sky more often and [14] recalls not only the airy atmosphere of the previous scene but, possibly, the true reason for her misery. Golaud takes Mélisande's hand and

16

Thomas Allen as Pelléas and Anne Howells as Mélisande in the Covent Garden production in 1978. (photo: Christina Burton)

Pelléas (Henry Gui) and Mélisande (Denise Duval) in the 1962 Glyndebourne production by Carl Ebert, designed by Beni Montrésor. (photo: Guy Gravett)

Debussy accompanies his fit of tenderness with impossibly delicate flutterings on flutes and upper strings. Golaud, we feel, cannot sustain such a mood. And sure enough, he notices that her ring is missing. He returns to a more urgent interrogation. In terror, she lies about where she lost it, telling Golaud she had been to a cave by the sea to collect shells for Golaud's little son Yniold; she dropped the ring and the tide came in before she could find it. Golaud insists she go and look for it immediately —that ring is worth more to him than all the rest of his possessions. Mélisande is frightened to go alone. Golaud shouts at her to take Pelléas. 'Pelléas will do anything you ask him. I know Pelléas better than you', at which pizzicato 'cellos and basses laugh sardonically. Mélisande goes out in tears.

The interlude, based almost entirely on [3] and [8] and wonderfully orchestrated to suggest the surging of the tide, takes us to the cave where Pelléas and Mélisande have gone to look for the ring, knowing of course that they will not find it. The music is vague and mysterious, almost aimless, until the moon comes out suddenly [19] and throws a flood of light into the cave, revealing three white-haired beggars lying asleep. The emotional expansiveness of [19] is abruptly contracted into [20], ostensibly because Mélisande is overwhelmed by the shock of seeing the beggars; but the curtailment mirrors the unwillingness of Pelléas and Mélisande openly to admit to the world or to each other any bond closer than friendship. They go out quietly and the orchestra fades on fragments of [8] and [19].

Until now no scene has opened on a character alone. Everything therefore has been presented in the form of relationships. In the first scene of Act Three the curtain rises to show one of the towers of the castle, in the window of which Mélisande is sitting alone, combing her hair and singing a ballad to herself [21], which Debussy sets not in a major or minor key, but in the Dorian mode (E minor but with C sharp and D natural). Pelléas comes along the path under the tower and they talk. Is it a love duet? Pelléas cannot reach Mélisande, but the quality of their conversation is more open now, less restrained, and the musical lines are allowed to flow. Pelléas exclaims, for the first time, at her beauty. She leans further and further out of the window so that he can touch her hand but just as they are about to make contact her hair falls over him. In a passage marked *'passionément contenu'* (with restrained passion) he takes hold of her hair, kisses it, winds it round his neck. She is afraid of falling, but he holds her fast. With growing passion [22] he ties her hair to the branches of the willow tree. As she cries, *'Tu m'as fait mal!'*, her doves are startled out of the tower and fly around

Henri-Bertrand Etcheverry as Golaud at the Opéra-Comique. (Bibliothèque de l'Opéra)

Jacques Jansen in 1940 in Geneva as Pelléas, the role with which he was asociated for 30 years.

them in the dark. The appearance of [3] high on the violins encourages us to identify them with the release of Mélisande's emotions; the doves, symbols of peace and of love, are like her, timid and unfathomable. Pelléas and Mélisande hear footsteps. It is Golaud, and [23] signifies his fatal jealousy. He upbraids them for their childish behaviour and takes Pelléas off with him.

For the first time, the interlude contains the themes of all three main characters — [2, 3, 8] — emphasising that the triangular tensions are now established and must eventually be resolved. Act three, scene two, is a masterpiece in the creation of fear; as Debussy wrote, 'enough to make the sanest heads swim'. Golaud takes Pelléas below the castle to the vaults. Why? We never know, but the atmosphere is laden with possibilities. Is Golaud trying merely to frighten Pelléas? Or has he something more permanent in mind? They see the stagnant lake from which an odour of death seeps into the castle as though it infects the very fabric of the building and the family who never leave it. 'One slip'. . . 'Do you see the abyss, Pelléas?'. . . 'It's stifling here'. . . And throughout the scene we hear the whole-tone scale [24], in which all steps are the same and through which there is no clear path. Flutes, harps and violins have all been silent during this scene. Now, in a justly famous passage of orchestral magic, they bring us up to the light and the clean smell of the sea, as the midday bells ring out. Golaud warns Pelléas that last night's behaviour must not be repeated. Mélisande is delicate and will soon be having her baby (and how intelligently Debussy underlines this statement with [3] harmonised as it was at the end of Act One, when Pelléas first offered his arm to Mélisande — *he* knows better than Golaud how delicate she is!). Pelléas must keep out of her way, without drawing attention to the fact.

The final scene of Act Three is set in front of the castle. Golaud takes his little boy Yniold on his knee and questions him about his step-mother and her relationship with Pelléas. In contrast to Golaud's tortuous harmonies, Yniold's are innocuous [25]. He tells 'the truth' as he sees it, but it is not the sort of truth Golaud can easily understand. Pelléas and Mélisande don't want the door open when they are together, Yniold tells him. Golaud is so determined to get to the bottom of this that he becomes impatient and Yniold begins to cry. Golaud promises him a quiver and some arrows and the investigation proceeds. The stylisation of Yniold's role comes direct from Maeterlinck's text, where his speech is larded with the phrase *'petit père'* — in all, 28 of them in the course of the scene. Setting the phrase gave Debussy nightmares, but he bravely did not cut any of them. The irritating effect they had on some of the early Paris audiences may be assumed to work on Golaud too. At least the rhythm of Yniold's *'petit père'* [26] is repeated in Golaud's outburst *'patience, mon Dieu, patience'* [27]. Golaud comes to the question of whether Pelléas and Mélisande have ever kissed each other. 'Yes' says Yniold, 'just like this', and kisses his father on the mouth. A light goes on in the window under which they are sitting [28], and the music modulates to F# major — the key of the end of Act One and of the love duet in Act Four. Debussy infuses a similar tenderness here. Though the audience cannot see into the room, we, like Golaud, imagine it from what Yniold says; and it could be argued that this exercise of our imagination makes what follows all the more shocking. Golaud lifts Yniold up to the window and asks him what he sees, and in the orchestra begin the galloping triplets that will take us through almost unchecked to the end of the Act. In short, Yniold sees nothing except that Pelléas and Mélisande are looking at the light. The horrors are in Golaud's mind. (Here 15 bars during which Golaud asks about the bed were cut on the censor's instructions. As they interrupt the triplet movement and include two more invocations to *'petit père'* perhaps they are no great loss.) Eventually Yniold begins to panic and threatens to scream. Golaud lets him down and they go off into the night.

Thomas Stewart as Golaud and Anne Howells as Mélisande at Covent Garden in 1978. (photo: Christina Burton)

The first scene of Act Four, set in a room in the castle, continues the agitation, but between Pelléas and Mélisande, though Golaud's shadow is ever-present; [29] suggests that Pelléas and Golaud may never be free of each other. Pelléas's father is recovering and has encouraged Pelléas to get away from the castle. He claims to see in his son's face a look of impending death. Pelléas and Mélisande agree to an assignation that evening by the well. They hear the sound of voices and Pelléas leaves before Arkel enters ([3] and [6] combined) and the scurrying semiquavers turn to more gentle triplets. In a long, measured speech Arkel tells Mélisande that with the recovery of Pelléas's father, life will return to the castle and that he sees her as opening a new era in its existence. He has felt great sympathy for her [30] and her youth and beauty console him as he draws nearer to death. The tail of [30] persists as [2] to mark Golaud's entrance. He has blood on his forehead. Mélisande offers to wipe it off but he repulses her and asks for his sword. She hands it to him and he looks in her eyes, to see . . . what? 'Nothing but innocence' says Arkel. Golaud takes up the theme of innocence with manic irony, and Debussy catches his mounting fury with restless orchestral textures — religious calm contrasting with rhythms of stabbing intensity. As his temper goes out of control, the triplets begin, reminding us of the end of Act Three. He seizes Mélisande by the hair and drags her along the floor. It is clear from his shouts of 'To the left, to the right: Absalom! Absalom!' that Mélisande has become a mere object, and so her theme is nowhere heard. The triplets are all. Suddenly Golaud goes calm and starts to maintain that none of this matters to him. Arkel does nothing to stop Golaud's violent behaviour but moralises on the misery of the human condition in general. For once, only Mélisande states the plain truth: 'He no longer loves me . . . I am not happy'.

The interlude that follows is the longest in the opera, as it perhaps needs to be in order to recollect and contemplate fully the horrors of what has passed, and to have time to make a natural transition to the innocence of Yniold, who carries the next scene by himself. He is discovered by the well in the park (last seen in Act Two, scene one) trying to move a large stone behind which his ball has got stuck. In some early performances this scene was omitted, possibly because Debussy felt it held up the momentum and because the symbolism is laid on rather thickly. Yniold's struggles with the intractable stone obviously match those of his father with life in general, and the sheep who pass offstage on their way 'not to the fold' prefigure the shedding of human blood. Yniold's music is dominated first by the *ostinato* representing the immovable stone [31], then by the triplets of the milling sheep (here Debussy adds to the symbolism by setting Yniold's questions 'Where are they going?' [32] to the accompaniment of Mélisande's *'Il fait sombre dans les jardins!'* 'The gardens seem enshrouded in night!' from Act One, scene three).

Night falls and Yniold leaves. Ushered in by dark, Mussorgskyan sounds [33] on low woodwind and strings Pelléas comes to keep his tryst with Mélisande. Common sense tells him he should finish matters while he has the chance, and leave without seeing her: the orchestra extend Mélisande's theme [3], breaking its circularity [34], but at once proceed to repeat the new phrase — Pelléas is caught by a larger destiny. He has decided he must see her just once more. He prepares himself to declare everything he has so far left unspoken. She enters and the long love duet begins.

As is the way with love duets, not a great deal happens that one can set out authoritatively in cold print. Instead the nuances multiply, with reminiscences of their earlier meeting by the well and a telling appearance of [2] as Pelléas warns her that in an hour's time the castle gates will be shut. He tells her he is leaving and the thought of separation impels him to an avowal of love [35]. Much has been made by the critics of the reticence of these unaccompanied declarations. But after all Pelléas and Mélisande are not Cavaradossi and Tosca, and Debussy is only following Maeterlinck's stage direction, *'Il l'embrasse brusquement'*. Pelléas's growing self-confidence is plain to hear shortly after this [36] in the passage with which Debussy began the composition of the opera in the autumn of 1893. Its traditional, rather solid texture may owe something to the fact that

Debussy had not yet worked himself fully into the ethos of the opera, but it turns out to suggest rather well the naïvety of Pelléas in expressing a passion new to him. The sound of the gates closing interrupts them and before long the dotted rhythms of Golaud portend tragedy. The music once more moves into triple metre for the climax and a new theme [37], a variation of [36], depicts heedless, desperate rapture. Golaud is watching and finally he hurls himself upon them and strikes Pelléas down with his sword. He then pursues Mélisande silently through the wood, the jealousy motif [23] telling its own story.

As mentioned earlier, Act Five of the play opens with a conversation between the castle servants. From them we learn that after killing Pelléas and wounding Mélisande Golaud turned his sword on himself, but has survived — hence Golaud's references to his own impending death in the second scene, which forms Act Five of the opera. It is set in a room in the castle and from large, dramatic, catastrophic gestures we move back to an intimate scale, as exemplified by the contraction of [3] to [38] with which the Act opens. The use of flute, clarinet, harp and strings reminds us of a time when all was well, but the hesitant nature of the music they play tells us that the time is now out of joint. Mélisande lies on the bed; Arkel, Golaud and the doctor confer in a corner of the room. The doctor has small hope of saving her but reassures Golaud that he must not feel responsible for her death. Mélisande wakes up and says she has never felt better; but the new theme [39] heard at this point on the oboe, and marked 'triste et très doucement expressif', indicates the truth. Arkel somewhat nervously tells her that Golaud is also in the room. Mélisande, far from being afraid, is surprised that he hasn't come near her of his own accord. During her conversation with Golaud, Debussy contrasts the desperate, ever-ranging questions from Golaud with Mélisande's calm fatalism by giving Golaud ever-ranging material, while to Mélisande he accords a calm formula heard three times in all [40] — Emmanuel calls it the 'pardon' theme, but in fact its plain harmonies signify as much as anything a refusal to be involved in Golaud's chromatic self-torturings: the distance between husband and wife is as great as ever.

Golaud asks to be left alone with her and from here he begins to indulge in a complex mélange of guilt, curiosity, jealousy and self-pity, caught by Debussy with a sure genius that defies detailed exposition; though we may once again note the reappearance of urgent triplet figures as the interrogation gets under way. The key phrase in Golaud's search is 'la vérité'. Mélisande swears to tell the truth, but because of the spiritual distance between her and Golaud the concept has no common meaning. Each time the phrase comes Debussy sets it differently, suggesting that, even for the individual, 'truth' changes from moment to moment. Arkel returns and from him we (and Mélisande) learn that she has had her child. He holds up the baby girl for her to see and to the accompaniment of [39] Mélisande speaks her last words. The serving women file into the room, unbidden, and stand along the walls. Golaud makes a brief show of authority in asking them what business they have to be there, but soon relapses into passivity. For the rest, one can only marvel at what Debussy has made out of almost nothing. Thematically [39] is the basis, together with [2] and [3], but the final pages —both a summary of past events and an intimation that the wheel of fate will go on turning — are among Debussy's finest achievements. When he played through the piano score to the assembled cast before rehearsals began, Mary Garden recalls, 'It was all very strange and unbearable. I closed my book and just listened to him, and as he played the death of Mélisande, I burst into the most awful sobbing. . . and. . . fled into the next room'. According to the best French traditions, by delicate means Debussy achieves a powerful end.

Maeterlinck and the Theatre

Alan Raitt

The reputations of writers are notoriously volatile, but few can have fluctuated as wildly as that of Maurice Maeterlinck. The early poems and tales of the young Belgian excited little notice in the heady climate of literary Paris in the late 1880's, but when he published his first play, *La Princesse Maleine*, in 1890, the critic Octave Mirbeau made him into an overnight celebrity by hailing it as superior to Shakespeare. From that moment on, his fame grew apace as plays, poems and essays continued to pour from his pen. His works commanded immense sales and were instantly translated into numerous other languages, his dramas were acted all over the world, his foreign tours were triumphal progresses, he was awarded the Nobel Prize for Literature in 1911, he was ennobled by the King of the Belgians in 1932, and the French Academy more than once contemplated bending its rules in order to have the honour of electing him. But by the time he died in 1949 at the age of 86, he was a profoundly lonely and unfashionable figure, and since then his once brilliant fame has suffered an almost total eclipse. The writings that used to delight and impress millions of readers are rarely in print, the plays remain unacted, and even specialists are reluctant to take him seriously. Were it not for the inspiration musicians derived from him, the man who achieved the remarkable feat of being, as someone has said, both the Edmond Rostand and the Albert Camus of his generation would today be no more than a forgotten curiosity in manuals of literary history.

No doubt the present total neglect is as unjustifiable as the original extraordinary infatuation. The discredit into which the weaker parts of his work have fallen has been unfairly extended to those writings which have some claim to permanent value, and the absurdly exaggerated praise once lavished on him has provoked an almost equally excessive denigration. The fact is that Maeterlinck's early plays, those written in the first half of the 1890's while the Symbolist movement was at its height, do have a distinctive style and atmosphere all of their own, and — despite their decidedly period air, with their mock medievalism and their moribund princesses — they still retain at least some of their power to move and disturb. After experimenting with a tissue of Gothic horrors in *La Princesse Maleine*, which is either Shakespearean or ridiculous according to the degree of indulgence with which one views it, Maeterlinck evolved a much simpler manner in which characters were stripped down to a few elemental impulses, plots became no more than outlines of archetypal situations, settings were vague and timeless, and language was more notable for what it hinted at than for what it put into words. *L'Intruse, Les Aveugles, Les Sept Princesses, Pelléas et Mélisande, Alladine et Palomides, Intérieur* and *La Mort de Tintagiles*, all written between 1890 and 1894, constitute the product of this manner, and remain Maeterlinck's most durable claim to fame.

Thereafter, his career began to veer off into a new direction. Conscious that the Symbolist movement was running into an impasse, that the public was wearying of effete idealistic pessimism, that he could not indefinitely exploit the narrow range of theatrical effects he had chosen, Maeterlinck attempted to extend his range by injecting more action into his dramas, by varying their tonality more, by making their characters more positive and more rounded, and by expounding his philosophy in an interminable series of discursive essays. Unfortunately, while this evolution enhanced his favour with readers and audiences alike, it also tended to turn him into a rather conventional if competent playwright and revealed him as a singularly woolly and obscurantist thinker. The sense of cosmic menace which had so impressively pervaded his early plays was now comfortably subsumed into a rather complacent acceptance of life, while the mysterious hinterland of their action was slowly swamped by a wash of prose as blandly mellifluous as it was vacuous. For another fifty years, Maeterlinck continued writing remorselessly, but though his sales held up with that vast public prepared to accept oracular obscurity for profundity, his impact on more discerning critics progressively diminished.

There were of course still genuine and deserved successes from time to time. His studies of the life of bees (1901), termites (1927) and ants (1930) may not have much scientific or philosophic weight, but they are fascinatingly readable. *Monna Vanna* (1901) is a solidly constructed historical drama; for all its coyness and pseudo-philosophical airs, *L'Oiseau bleu* (1908) has undeniable charm and ingenuity; *Le Bourgmestre de Stilemonde* (1919) is a powerful manifestation of wartime patriotism. But there is never enough thrust or originality in the later Maeterlinck for his works to appear as anything other than an increasingly inadequate response to the tragedies and complexities of the modern world — indeed, his involvement with that world dwindled to an occasional and unfortunate sympathy with fascist dictatorships. Moreover, his preoccupation with money and his creature comforts, as well as his predilection for mundane activities such as eating, drinking, womanising, motorcycling and boxing ended by arousing suspicions that ultimately his commitment to things of the mind was little more than skin deep. There seems little likelihood that there will ever be any major rehabilitation of Maeterlinck's post-1894 writings.

The early theatre is however another matter. The impression of man as a puny creature threatened by forces he can neither control nor comprehend perhaps looks forward to the universe of Kafka. The anguished inarticulacy of the protagonists may be seen as a prefiguration of Beckett's struggle with the tragic inadequacy of language. Yeats's theatre and Wilde's *Salome* undoubtedly owe something to the dramatic perspectives Maeterlinck opened up in these dramas. If his near-contemporary Paul Claudel is by far the more individual writer and the more powerful voice, it is arguable that it was Maeterlinck more than anyone else who captured the quintessence of Symbolism on the stage —its poetic imagery, its rejection of the values of materialism, its striving towards a reality beyond that of everyday perceptions, its evocation of the evanescent and the impalpable, its transmutation of language into something capable of infinite modulation, its preference for suggestion rather than statement. Therein lies perhaps such greatness as he has —and there too lies the secret of the extraordinary fascination his works have held for musicians.

For Debussy's *Pelléas et Mélisande* is only the most famous of the innumerable musical works inspired by Maeterlinck's pen. At least a score of operas have been based on his plays, to say nothing of the overtures, the symphonic poems, the songs, the sets of incidental music. From 1891 to 1930 and even beyond, the flow of Maeterlinck-derived compositions was almost unceasing. The composers who fell under his spell include figures as diverse and as distinguished as Fauré, Sibelius, Schoenberg, Webern, Rachmaninov, Martinů and Honegger, and among them are representatives of almost every nationality — Britons, Italians, Czechs, Dutchmen, Portuguese, Swedes, Russians, Americans and Austrians, as well as the Belgians and Frenchmen one might expect. Clearly, at one time Maeterlinck appealed to musicians of all countries and all tendencies more than any other contemporary writer — indeed, such universal enthusiasm must be a unique phenomenon in the history of music. There was even a symphonic poem suggested, not by one of the plays or poems, but by a collection of essays. . . How can one account for this near-unanimous acclaim for an author who is far from being another Shakespeare or Victor Hugo, those other favourite sources of opera

A design by Valentine Hugo for the 1947 Paris production. (Royal College of Music)

libretti and musical inspiration generally?

The first thing to be said is that Maeterlinck's spare, uncluttered dramaturgy is exceptionally well suited to operatic ends. The situations he depicts are so basic, so close to the heart of the human condition, that they require little in the way of exposition or explanation. They thus lend themselves to an almost continuously lyrical treatment; there is no need for those passages of narration and information which usually seem resistant to musical settings. One emotional state merges into another by a kind of organic development, with few interruptions from external events, so that the composer is free to concentrate on the development of his themes, to the exclusion of alien elements.

Secondly, Maeterlinck's use of recurrent themes and images is a gift to post-Wagnerian musicians. In *Pelléas et Mélisande*, the repeated references to the fountain, the ring or Mélisande's hair offer obvious opportunities for thematic links, just as the frequent repetition of words and phrases in the dialogue is a clear incitement to the elaboration of musical echo effects. Even composers who did not wish systematically to adopt the Wagnerian idea of the *Leitmotiv* were quick to realise how readily this aspect of Maeterlinck's dramatic technique could be exploited in purely musical terms.

The refusal of any form of realism in his theatre was a further encouragement to musicians in search of suitable libretti. Generally speaking, the vogue for realistic and naturalistic subjects in the post-Romantic theatre had held little attraction for operatic composers. With few exceptions, they had taken the view that the gap between the realistic convention in drama and the necessarily non-realistic convention of opera constituted an insuperable obstacle to the adaptation of such subjects. The result was that they tended to turn to contemporary dramatists only for comic or light opera, and for grand opera went on plundering the Romantic theatre, itself seriously outdated as literature. Maeterlinck presented them with an entirely new opening: plays which were modern in their inspiration but at the same time admirably suited in their remoteness, their lack of explicitness in setting and expression, to the perspective of the operatic stage.

Finally, and most importantly, Maeterlinck's language itself had unmistakable musical qualities. It had the beauty and evocativeness of poetry without inflicting on the musician the Procrustean constraints of regular rhyme and metre, and it constantly seemed to allude to feelings too tenuous to be put into words. Maeterlinck more than anyone else inaugurates the theatre of the unspoken, and the silences in his dramas are always pregnant with emotion. To the musician, such an attitude to language was a boon. Instead of having to compete with words which were wholly self-sufficient, he was able to use music to complement the dialogue, to tease out its overtones and nuances, to heighten its oblique and allusive emotive effects, to give the impression that language was an incomplete and inadequate medium, which could only attain its full power when allied to its sister art. It is not only because of Debussy that when we read Maeterlinck's texts today, we feel that they are crying out for the support of music: that is something which was inherent in them from the outset and which was as apparent to his contemporaries as it is to us.

Not the least paradox of this situation is that Maeterlinck himself was tone-deaf and initially somewhat resentful at the intrusion of music into his plays (it was only when he realised the financial advantages it could bring that he started writing works such as *Ariane et Barbe-bleue* and *Soeur Béatrice* with opera specifically in mind). When *Pelléas et Mélisande* was first produced at the Opéra-Comique in 1902, Maeterlinck quarrelled violently with Debussy, wanted to fight a duel with him, and threatened to beat him up with his stick, and it was not until 1920 that he consented to attend a performance (when he had the good grace to admit that it was the first time that he had entirely understood his own play). Had he been more musical, it is quite possible that he would never have written as he did, since he might well have felt that music was a more appropriate vehicle than language for the effects he was aiming to produce. Paul Valéry claimed that the unifying factor in the Symbolist movement was the desire of poets to reclaim from music that which rightly belonged to them. Curiously, those who were most successful in that aim were those who, like Verlaine or Maeterlinck, had little real feeling for music as an autonomous art — and the musicians soon saw how in their turn they could recover the disputed territory which the men of letters had sought to usurp.

So it is that today the name of Maeterlinck is inseparably associated with music, whereas it means little in literature. The poet, who prided himself on being a guide and philosopher, would have been profoundly shocked at this development. To the rest of us, it seems eminently fair. Debussy and the other composers whom he inspired undoubtedly detected the outstanding quality of his works, namely, their affinity with music, and took full advantage of it. If *Pelléas et Mélisande* is one of the summits of modern opera, it is in no small measure because Maeterlinck unwittingly provided a text that was already halfway towards being a musical score. It is a considerable tribute to him that, whatever his other shortcomings, he should have made it possible for a masterwork to come into being.

Profound or Pretentious?

Reactions to the play and the opera

Nicholas John

The Symbolist movement in all the arts won fervent supporters and provoked much satirical criticism. Maeterlinck remained in many ways the stolid Belgian *bourgeois* he had been brought up; Georgette Leblanc, on the other hand, the actress-singer with whom he shared twenty-five years of his life, was altogether more flamboyant. She had first fallen in love with him by reading his works, and to impress him she draped a room for him entirely in black, with silver ornaments, only to find that he preferred to sit and smoke in an ordinary room. When he proposed, she commented:

> How could one descend from Paradise to call at the registry office! . . . The idea of marriage never occurred to me for one moment until the day when Maeterlinck spoke of it . . . At the first word, he saw me in such perfect bewilderment that he did not insist.

Maeterlinck's play was first given in Paris at a matinée in 1893. The costumes were based on Memlinc's paintings; the set, seen through a thin gauze, was inspired by Walter Crane's illustrations. The reception was sympathetic because the audience was full of admirers such as Mallarmé — and Debussy. Some months later, however, at the first Belgian performance, a friend reported:

> The whole legion was there to defend the work of Maeterlinck against the eternal enemy, the *bourgeois*, who also had come in a great procession. . . . The hatred of the *bourgeois* for all that is ideal, great, and beautiful in Maeterlinck is really fierce. Sublime passages were laughed at; a section of the public even went so far as to take advantage of the darkness to imitate the noise of kissing in the great love scene of Act IV. That lovely scene of the sheep told by little Yniold which is like a sudden pastoral, a distant melancholic air on a flute between two sombre scenes, was welcomed by gusts of laughter. And it was played by a marvellous young girl.

In 1895, Maeterlinck travelled to London for a season of contemporary European drama which also included Ibsen's plays. The costumes were lost in transit. Because it was a Saturday afternoon, and the shops were shutting, it is said that Pelléas had to wear the kilt, sporran and glengarry lent by a Scotsman whom Maeterlinck saw in the street. The play made little impression then but it was given in English for the first time in 1898 with success, and Arthur Symons reviewed a subsequent revival:

> *Pelléas and Mélisande* is the most beautiful of Maeterlinck's plays, and to say this is to say that it is the most beautiful contemporary play. Maeterlinck's theatre of marionettes, who are at the same time children and spirits, at once more simple and more abstract than real people, is the reaction of the imagination against the wholly prose theatre of Ibsen, into which life comes nakedly, cruelly, subtly, but without distinction, without poetry. Maeterlinck has invented plays which are pictures, in which the crudity of action is subdued into misty outlines. People with strange names, living in impossible places, where there are only woods and fountains, and towers by the sea-shore, and ancient castles, where there are no towns, and where the common crowd of the world is shut out of sight and hearing, move like quiet ghosts across the stage, mysterious to us and

not less mysterious to one another. They are all lamenting because they do not know, because they cannot understand, because their own souls are so strange to them, and each other's souls like pitiful enemies, giving deadly wounds unwillingly. They are always in dread, because they know that nothing is certain in the world or in their own hearts, and they know that love most often does the work of hate and that hate is sometimes tenderer than love. In *Pelléas and Mélisande* we have two innocent lovers, to whom love is guilt; we have blind vengeance, aged and helpless wisdom; we have the conflict of passions fighting in the dark, destroying what they desire most in the world. And out of this tragic tangle Maeterlinck has made a play which is too full of beauty to be painful. We feel an exquisite sense of pity, so impersonal as to be almost healing, as if our own sympathy had somehow set right the wrongs of the play.

And this play, translated with delicate fidelity by Mr Mackail, was acted yesterday afternoon by Mrs Patrick Campbell, Mr Martin Harvey, and others, to the accompaniment of M. Fauré's music, and in the midst of scenery which gave a series of beautiful pictures, worthy of the play. Mrs Campbell, in whose art there is so much that is pictorial, has never been so pictorial as in the character of Mélisande. At the beginning I thought she was acting with more effort and less effect than in the original performance; but as the play went on she abandoned herself more and more simply to the part she was acting, and in the death scene had a kind of quiet, poignant, reticent perfection. A plaintive figure out of tapestry, a child out of a nursery tale, she made one feel at once the remoteness and the humanity of this waif of dreams, the little princess who does [not?] know that it is wrong to love. In the great scene by the fountain in the park, Mrs Campbell expressed the supreme unconsciousness of passion, both in face and voice, as no other English actress could have done; in the death scene she expressed the supreme unconsciousness of innocence with the same beauty and the same intensity. Her palpitating voice, in which there is something like the throbbing of a wounded bird, seemed to speak the simple and beautiful words as if they had never been said before. And that beauty and strangeness in her, which make her a work of art in herself, seemed to find the one perfect opportunity for their expression. The only actress on our stage whom we go to see as we would go to see a work of art, she acts Pinero and the rest as if under a disguise. Here, dressed in wonderful clothes of no period, speaking delicate, almost ghostly words, she is herself, her rarer self. And Mr Martin Harvey, who can be so simple, so passionate, so full of the warmth of charm, seemed until almost the end of the play to have lost the simple fervour which he had once shown in the part of Pelléas; he posed, spoke without sincerity, was conscious of little but his attitudes. But in the great love scene by the fountain in the park he had recovered sincerity, he forgot himself, remembering Pelléas; and that great love scene was acted with a sense of the poetry and a sense of the human reality of the thing, as no-one on the London stage but Mr Harvey and Mrs Campbell could have acted it. No-one else, except Mr Arliss as the old servant, was good; the acting was not sufficiently monotonous, with that fine monotony which is part of the secret of Maeterlinck. These busy actors occupied themselves in making points, instead of submitting passively to the passing through them of profound emotions, and the betrayal of these emotions in a few, reticent, and almost unwilling words.

In 1893 Debussy secured Maeterlinck's permission to set the play to music and, incidentally, to perform it how, when and where Debussy wished. Nine years later he played the completed score to the author. Georgette Leblanc maintained that it was then assumed she would sing Mélisande. When Debussy and Albert Carré, the director of the Opéra-Comique, offered the part to Mary Garden, the then little known Scots-American soprano, Maeterlinck was outraged. He threatened Debussy with violence and publicly wished 'the opera would be a prompt and resounding flop'. Abusive leaflets were handed around outside the theatre; nicknames such as 'Pelléas et Médisances' were invented. Nevertheless, Mary Garden, whose slight accent served her perfectly for Mélisande, led an excellent cast, superbly conducted by André Messager. Despite reservations in the press, the opera was taken up by the fashionable and the discerning public and played to good houses.

The cave by the sea designed by Ronsin for the first production. (Stuart-Liff Collection)

Proust was among those who counted themselves as 'Pelléastres'; Debussy's music inspired the character of Vinteuil in *A la recherche du temps perdu*. One character observes she can never hear the opera without catching hay-fever. While Reynaldo Hahn was in Russia during 1911, Proust wrote to him describing how he satisfied his sudden craving for music by subscribing to the Theatrephone. By this private telephone exchange company he could obtain relays of live performances while lying in bed at home — and so he listened to *Pelléas*. A fragment of a pastiche of *Pelléas* has recently been published in *The Notebooks of Marcel Proust* (edited by Philip Kolb). I am indebted for the following extract to M. Pierre Macherey in whose *montage* 'Proust et Pelléas' for l'Avant-Scène (Opéra), 9, it appears.

You were wrong to leave that hat! You will never find it!

Vous avez eu tort de laisser ce chapeau! Vous ne le retrouverez jamais!

PELLEAS

Why will I never find it?

Pourquoi ne le retrouverai-je jamais?

MARKEL

One never finds anything again . . . here . . . it is lost forever.

On ne retrouve jamais rien . . . ici . . . Il est perdu pour toujours.

PELLEAS

As we go, we will find another which looks like it!

En nous en allant, nous en prendrons un – qui lui ressemble!

MARKEL

There are none which look like it!

Il n'y en a pas qui lui ressemble!

PELLEAS

What was it like then?

Comment était-il donc?

MARKEL
(*very softly*)

It was a poor little hat like everyone wears! No one could tell whose it was . . . It looked as though it came from the end of the world!

C'était un pauvre petit chapeau comme en porte tout le monde! Personne n'aurait pu dire de chez qui il venait . . . Il avait l'air de venir du bout du monde!

Now, we should not look for it any longer because we will not find it.

Maintenant, il ne faut plus le chercher car nous ne le retrouverons pas.

PELLEAS

It seems to me that my head is going to be cold forever. It is very cold outside. It is winter! If only the sun had not yet set. Why has someone left the window open? The atmosphere in there was heavy and poisoned; several times I thought I was going to feel ill. And now all the fresh air in the world!

Il me semble que ma tête commence à avoir froid pour toujours. Il fait un grand froid dehors. C'est l'hiver! Si encore le soleil n'était pas couché. Pourquoi avait-on laissé la fenêtre ouverte? Il faisait, là-dedans, une atmosphère lourde et empoisonnée; j'ai cru plusieurs fois que j'allais me trouver mal. Et maintenant tout l'air de toute la terre!

MARKEL

Your face, Pelléas, is serious and tearful like those who have had colds for a long time! Let us go. We will not find it. Someone who does not come from here will have taken it and God knows where it is by now. It is too late. All the other hats have left. We could no longer take another. It is a terrible thing, Pelléas. But it is not your fault.

Vous avez, Pelléas, le visage grave et plein de larmes (de) ceux qui sont enrhumés pour longtemps! Allons-nous en. Nous ne le retrouverons pas. Quelqu'un qui n'est pas d'ici l'aura emporté et Dieu sait où il est en ce moment. Il est trop tard. Tous les autres chapeaux sont partis. Nous ne pourrons plus en prendre un autre. C'est une chose terrible, Pelléas. Mais ce n'est pas votre faute.

PELLEAS

What is that noise?

Quel est ce bruit?

MARKEL

That is the carriages leaving.

Ce sont les voitures qui partent.

PELLEAS

Why are they leaving?

Pourquoi partent-elles?

MARKEL

We will have scared them. They knew that we are going a very long way from here and they have left. They will never come back.

Nous les aurons effrayées. Elles savaient que nous en allons très loin d'ici et elles sont parties. Elles ne reviendront jamais.

Clarence Whitehill
Golaud at the Met.
première.
(Met. Archives)

Lucrezia Bori,
Mélisande at the
1925 Met. première.
(Met. Archives)

At the New York première six years later, the reception was described as one of:

> rather amazed, respectful and intelligent attention, of courteous and hearty appreciation of the remarkable work of the artists rather than of spontaneous enthusiasm for the work itself . . . although the applause was ample.

In 1911 Maeterlinck's friend, the impresario Henry Russell, invited both him and Debussy to collaborate on a staging of the opera at the Boston Grand Opera House. Georgette Leblanc was to sing Mélisande — the forbidden role — and, to fill the house, he invented a series of rumours that Maeterlinck was travelling incognito with her and had laid a bet that he could land without being spotted by journalists. Despite his efforts, the season was not, however, a box-office success.

Not until 1920, two years after Debussy's death, did Maeterlinck attend the opera. He then wrote to Mary Garden . . .

> For the first time I have entirely understood my own play, and because of you.

*George Shirley (Pelléas) with Elizabeth
Söderström (Mélisande) at Covent Garden
in 1969. (photo: Zoe Dominic)*

*Jerome Hines (Arkel) and Teresa Stratas)
(Mélisande) at the Met. (Met. Archives;
photo: J. Hefferman)*

Thematic Guide

Some of the musical themes in the opera have been identified here. They are numbered in square brackets for easy reference in the articles and the libretto.

The lower stave in examples [7], [10] and [26] shows the different note values of the English text.

[1] Très modéré

[2] Golaud — Très modéré

[3] Mélisande — Très modéré

[4] Très modéré

[5] Modéré

[6] Royalty ? (Modéré)

[7] GENEVIEVE (Modéré)

Je ne sais ni son à - ge, ni qui elle est, ni d'ou el - le
I know nei-ther her age —, nor who she is, nor where she

vient et je n'o-se pas l'in-ter -ro -ger,
comes from and I dare not ask her,

[8] *Pelleas*

(Anime)

[9]

Plus modere et tres expressif

[10] PELLEAS

Sans lenteur

et ce - pen - dant elle est si cal - me mainte-nant!
and yet the sea is ve - ry calm this evening . . .

[11] CHORUS

En animant

Ho - e! Hisse ho-e! ho e!
Hisse
Ho -e! Ho-e! Ho - e!

[12]

(Lent)

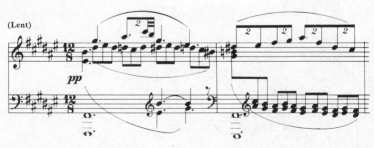

34

[13]

(Lent)

[14]

(Mouvemente)

[15]

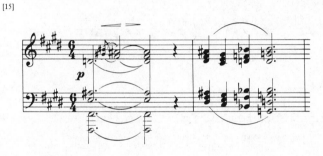

[16]

Modéré, en animant

[17]   *The Ring*

[18]

Modéré

Doux et calme

[20]

[21] MELISANDE

Modéré et librement

Mes longs che - veux des - cen - dent jusqu'au seuil de la   tour
My hair's so   long   it   rea - ches down to the foot of the   tower

[22]

Modéré

p *très expressif*

[23]

Modéré

[24]

Lourd et sombre

[25]

Modéré

[26] YNIOLD

Modéré

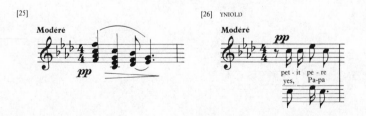

pet - it   pè - re
yes,   Pa-pa

GOLAUD

Retenu

pa - ti - en - ce,   mon Dieu, pa - ti - en - ce,
give me pat -ience,   my God, give me pat - ience ...

[28]

Dans le mouv^t. anime mais sans rigeur

très doux et
très expressif

[29]

Animé et agite

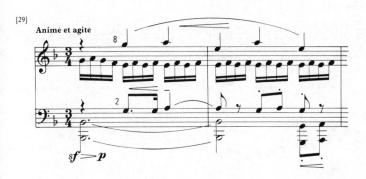

[30]

Modere

doux et expressif

[31]

Modere

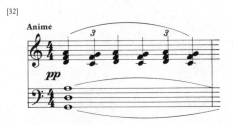

[32]

Anime

Pelléas & Mélisande

Lyric Drama in five acts and twelve scenes

Music by Claude Debussy
Libretto adapted from the play by Maurice Maeterlinck
English translation by Hugh Macdonald

Pelléas et Mélisande was first performed at the Opéra-Comique on April 30, 1902. It was first heard in America at the Manhattan Opera House on February 19, 1908. The first performance in England was at Covent Garden on May 21, 1909.

This translation of the opera libretto was commissioned by English National Opera for the 1981 production at the London Coliseum by Harry Kupfer.

The right-hand column gives the text of Maeterlinck's play *Pelléas et Mélisande*. Passages which Debussy omitted in his libretto are given in square brackets. Alterations which Debussy made to Maeterlinck's text (excepting repetitions and insignificant changes) are given in the footnotes. The left-hand column gives the singing translation of the text by Hugh Macdonald, with translations of the passages in the play which were omitted by Debussy given in square brackets. It should be noted that Maeterlinck revised his play in the course of its many editions, and that Debussy used the original 1893 text. This differs in many places from that to be found in Maeterlinck's *Collected Theatre*, for example, the most important alteration being Mélisande's song in Act Three.

The numbers in square brackets refer to the Thematic Guide. The stage directions are direct translations of those in the play and do not necessarily represent any actual production of the opera.

CHARACTERS
in order of singing

Golaud *Arkel's grandson*	*baritone*
Mélisande	*soprano*
Geneviève *mother of Golaud and Pelléas*	*mezzo-soprano*
Arkel *King of Allemonde*	*bass*
Pelléas *Arkel's grandson*	*baritone/tenor**
The little Yniold *Golaud's son by a*	
former marriage	*soprano*
A shepherd	*bass*
A doctor	*bass*

Servants, beggars.

* In fact, Debussy wrote Pelléas for his own vocal range, which is technically known as 'baryton-Martin'.

Act One

[¹**Scene One.** *The castle gate.*

SERVANTS
(*within*)

Open the gate! Open the gate!

Ouvrez la porte! Ouvrez la porte!

PORTER

Who's there? Why do you have to
wake me? Go out by the side doors,
go out by the side doors! There
are several . . .

Qui est là? Pourquoi venez-vous
m'éveiller? Sortez par les petites
portes; sortez par les petites portes;
il y en a assez! . . .

A SERVANT
(*within*)

We've come to wash the gateway and
scrub the steps. Open up! Open up!

Nous venons laver le seuil, la porte
et le perron; ouvrez donc! ouvrez donc!

ANOTHER SERVANT
(*within*)

Today's the great day!

Il y aura de grands événements!

THIRD SERVANT

There's to be a celebration! Open
up at once! . . .

Il y aura de grandes fêtes! Ouvrez
vite! . . .

SERVANTS

Open up! Open up!

Ouvrez donc! ouvrez donc!

PORTER

Wait! Wait! I don't know if I'll
be able to open it. It never
opens. Wait till it gets light . . .

Attendez! attendez! Je ne sais pas si
je pourrai l'ouvrir . . . Elle ne
s'ouvre jamais . . . Attendez qu'il
fasse clair . . .

FIRST SERVANT

It's light enough outside. I can
see the sun through the cracks . . .

Il fait assez clair au dehors; je vois
le soleil par les fentes . . .

PORTER

Here are the keys . . . Oh, listen
to the bolts and locks grinding!
Give me a hand, give me a hand!

Voici les grandes clefs . . . Oh! comme
ils grincent, les verrous et les
serrures . . . Aidez-moi! aidez-moi! . . .

SERVANTS

We're pulling, we're pulling . . .

Nous tirons, nous tirons . . .

SECOND SERVANT

It won't open . . .

Elle ne s'ouvrira pas . . .

FIRST SERVANT

Ah ha! It's opening! It's opening
bit by bit!

Ah! ah! Elle s'ouvre! elle s'ouvre
lentement!

PORTER

Listen to it squeaking! It'll
wake everyone up!

Comme elle crie! Elle éveillera tout
le monde . . .

---

¹ [This whole scene is omitted from the opera]

SECOND SERVANT
(appearing in the gateway)

Oh, look! It's already light out there!	Oh! qu'il fait déjà clair au dehors!

FIRST SERVANT

The sun's up over the sea!	Le soleil se lève sur la mer!

PORTER

It's open . . . It's wide open! . . .	Elle est ouverte . . . Elle est grande ouverte! . . .

(All the servants appear in the gateway and pass through.)

FIRST SERVANT

I'll wash the entrance first . . .	Je vais d'abord laver le seuil . . .

SECOND SERVANT

We'll never be able to clean all this.	Nous ne pourrons jamais nettoyer tout ceci.

OTHER SERVANTS

Fetch some water! Fetch some water!	Apportez l'eau! apportez l'eau!

PORTER

That's it, that's it. Pour out the water, spill out all the waters of the Flood. You'll never finish . . .]	Oui, oui; versez l'eau, versez toute l'eau du déluge; vous n'en viendrez jamais à bout . . .]

[1]**Scene Two.** *A forest. As the curtain rises Mélisande is discovered by a spring.* [1] *Enter Golaud.* [2, 3]

GOLAUD

I shall never find my way out of this forest. Heaven knows how far this animal has led me . . . I had the impression it was mortally wounded . . . Yes, here are traces of blood. But the beast itself is nowhere to be seen; indeed I fear I have lost my way, and my hounds will never find me here . . . I must try to retrace my steps . . . Someone's weeping? Oh! oh! Who is that beside the spring? Is that a girl there weeping by the water?	Je ne pourrai plus sortir de cette forêt. – Dieu sait jusqu'où cette bête m'a mené. Je croyais cependant l'avoir blessée à mort; et voici des traces de sang. Mais maintenant, je l'ai perdue de vue; je crois que je me suis perdu moi-même – et mes chiens ne me retrouvent plus – je vais revenir sur mes pas . . . –j'entends pleurer . . . Oh! oh! qu'y a-t-il là au bord de l'eau? . . . Une petite fille qui pleure au bord de l'eau?

[4]

(He coughs.)

She has not heard me . . . I cannot see her face . . .	Elle ne m'entend pas. Je ne vois pas son visage.

(He approaches Mélisande and touches her shoulder.)

Why are you weeping?	Pourquoi pleures-tu?

(Mélisande trembles, starts, and is about to run away.)

Don't be afraid. You have nothing to fear. Why are you weeping here, all alone?	N'ayez pas peur. Vous n'avez rien à craindre. Pourquoi pleurez-vous, ici, toute seule?

MELISANDE

Don't touch me! Don't touch me!	Ne me touchez pas! ne me touchez pas!

GOLAUD

Don't be afraid. I will do you no harm! Oh, you are so beautiful!	N'ayez pas peur . . . Je ne vous ferai pas . . . Oh! vous êtes belle!

MELISANDE

Don't touch me! Don't touch me! Or I shall throw myself in the water!	Ne me touchez pas! ou je me jette à l'eau! . . .

---

[1] Scene One of the opera. The word 'fontaine' describes the scene both here and in Act Two, scene one, although in English one is, traditionally, a pool or spring, while the other is a well.

GOLAUD

I shall not touch you ... You see, I will stay where I am by this tree. Don't be afraid. Has someone wronged you?

Je ne vous touche pas ... Voyez, je resterai ici, contre l'arbre. N'ayez pas peur. Quelqu'un vous a-t-il fait du mal?

MELISANDE

Oh yes! Yes! Yes! ...

Oh! oui! oui! oui! ...

(She sobs deeply.)

GOLAUD

Tell me, who has done you wrong?

Qui est-ce qui vous a fait du mal?

MELISANDE

Everyone! Everyone!

Tous! tous!

GOLAUD

And what wrong have they done?

Quel mal vous a-t-on fait?

MELISANDE

I don't want to tell you ... No, I cannot tell you ...

Je ne veux pas le dire! je ne peux pas le dire! ...

GOLAUD

Come, don't stay here weeping like this. Where is your home?

Voyons; ne pleurez pas ainsi. D'où venez-vous?

MELISANDE

I've run away! Run away! Run away!

Je me suis enfuie! ... enfuie ...

GOLAUD

Yes, but where have you run away from?

Oui; mais d'où vous êtes-vous enfuie?

MELISANDE

I am lost! Lost! Oh! Oh! Yes, I am lost ... This is not my home ... I was not born here ...

Je suis perdue! ... perdue! ... Oh! oh! perdue ici ... Je ne suis pas d'ici ... Je ne suis pas née là ...

GOLAUD

Where is your home? Where do you come from?

D'où êtes-vous? Où êtes-vous née?

MELISANDE

Oh! oh! far from here ... far ... far ...

Oh! oh! loin d'ici ... loin ... loin ...

GOLAUD

What is that glittering there down in the [5] water?

Qu'est-ce qui brille ainsi au fond de l'eau?

MELISANDE

Oh, where? Ah! It is the crown that he gave me. I was weeping, it fell in!

Où donc? – Ah! c'est la couronne qu'il m'a donnée. Elle est tombée en pleurant.

GOLAUD

A crown? And who was it gave you a crown? I'll see if I can reach it ...

Une couronne? – Qui est-ce qui vous a donnée une couronne? – Je vais essayer de la prendre ...

MELISANDE

No! No! I don't want it! I don't want it! I would much rather die ... die now at once! ...

Non, non; je n'en veux plus! Je préfère mourir tout de suite ...

GOLAUD

I could easily reach down and get it out ... The water is not very deep.

Je pourrais la retirer facilement. L'eau n'est pas très profonde.

42

MELISANDE

I don't want it! If you get it I would throw myself in!

Je n'en veux plus! Si vous la retirez, je me jette à sa place! . . .

GOLAUD

No, no, I will leave it alone. And yet I could reach it without any trouble. It looks very beautiful. Was it long ago that you ran away?

Non, non; je la laisserai là. On pourrait la prendre sans peine cependant. Elle semble très belle. – Y a-t-il longtemps que vous avez fui?

MELISANDE

Yes . . . Who are you?

Oui . . . Qui êtes-vous?

GOLAUD

I am Prince Golaud, grandson of old Arkel, [6] King of Allemonde.

Je suis le prince Golaud – le petit-fils d'Arkel, le vieux roi d'Allemonde . . .

MELISANDE

Oh, your hair is already turning grey.

Oh! vous avez déjà les cheveux gris . . .

GOLAUD

A little, here by the temples.

Oui; quelques-uns, ici, près des tempes . . .

MELISANDE

And your beard as well. Why do you look at me like that?

Et la barbe aussi . . . Pourquoi me regardez-vous ainsi?

GOLAUD

It's your eyes I am looking at. Do you ever close your eyes?

Je regarde vos yeux. – Vous ne fermez jamais les yeux?

MELISANDE

Yes, yes, I close them at night.

Si, si; je les ferme la nuit . . .

GOLAUD

Why do you look so bewildered?

Pourquoi avez-vous l'air si étonnée?

MELISANDE

Are you a giant?

Vous êtes un géant?

GOLAUD

I'm a man like any other.

Je suis un homme comme les autres . . .

MELISANDE

Why did you come here?

Pourquoi êtes-vous venu ici?

GOLAUD

I have no idea. – I was hunting in the forest. And I was following a boar. Then I lost my way . . . You seem very young. How old are you?

Je n'en sais rien moi-même. Je chassais dans la forêt. Je poursuivais un sanglier. Je me suis trompé de chemin. – Vous avez l'air très jeune. Quel âge avez-vous?

MELISANDE

I'm feeling cold.

Je commence à avoir froid . . .

GOLAUD

Would you like to come with me?

Voulez-vous venir avec moi?

MELISANDE

No, no, I'll stay here.

Non, non; je reste ici . . .

GOLAUD

You cannot stay here all alone in the forest, you cannot stay here alone in the wood all night . . . What is your name?

Vous ne pouvez pas rester ici toute seule. Vous ne pouvez pas rester ici toute la nuit . . . Comment vous nommez-vous?

Mélisande.

Mélisande.

GOLAUD

You cannot stay here alone, Mélisande. Come with me . . .

Vous ne pouvez pas rester ici, Mélisande. Venez avec moi . . .

MELISANDE

I'll stay here . . .

Je reste ici . . .

GOLAUD

You never know what may happen . . . all night long . . . all alone here. You cannot do it, Mélisande, come, give me your hand . . .

Vous aurez peur, toute seule. On ne sait pas ce qu'il y a ici . . . Toute la nuit . . . toute seule . . . ce n'est pas possible. Mélisande, venez, donnez-moi la main . . .

MELISANDE

Oh! Don't touch me!

Oh! ne me touchez pas! . . .

GOLAUD

Don't be alarmed . . . I'll not touch you again! But come with me. The night will be very dark and very cold. Come with me . . .

Ne criez pas . . . Je ne vous toucherai plus. Mais venez avec moi. La nuit sera très noire et très froide. Venez avec moi . . .

MELISANDE

Where are you going?

Où allez-vous? . . .

GOLAUD

I do not know . . . I too am lost . . .

Je ne sais pas . . . Je suis perdu aussi . . .

(*They go out.*)

Scene Three[1]. *A room in the castle. Arkel and Geneviève are discovered.*

GENEVIEVE

This is what he has written to his brother Pelléas: "One evening I found her in tears by the side of a spring, in the forest where I'd lost my way. I know neither her age nor [7] who she is, nor where she comes from, and I dare not ask her, for she must have suffered some terrible misfortune. And if you ask her what happened, she bursts into tears like a child and starts sobbing so bitterly that one is fearful for her. [Just as I came upon her by the spring, a golden crown had slipped from her hair and fallen into the water. She was dressed, moreover, as a princess, even though her clothes were torn by brambles.] It is now six months since I made her my wife, yet I know nothing more than I knew the day that I found her. Meanwhile, my dear Pelléas, whom I love more than a brother, even though we are not sons of the same father, have everything ready for my return. I know my mother will gladly and freely forgive me. But [I fear the king, our venerable grandfather,] I fear Arkel despite his loving heart, [for by this strange marriage I have thwarted all his political plans and I fear that Mélisande's beauty, in

Voici ce qu'il écrit à son frère Pelléas: "Un soir je l'ai trouvée tout en pleurs au bord d'une fontaine, dans la forêt où je m'étais perdu. Je ne sais ni son âge, ni qui elle est, ni d'où elle vient et je n'ose pas l'interroger, car elle doit avoir eu une grande épouvante, et quand on lui demande ce qui lui est arrivé, elle pleure tout à coup comme un enfant et sanglote si profondément qu'on a peur. [Au moment où je l'ai trouvée près des sources, une couronne d'or avait glissé de ses cheveux, et était tombée au fond de l'eau. Elle était d'ailleurs vêtue comme une princesse, bien que ses vêtements fussent déchirés par les ronces.] Il y a maintenant six mois que je l'ai épousée et je n'en sais pas plus qu'au jour de notre rencontre. En attendant, mon cher Pelléas, toi que j'aime plus qu'un frère, bien que nous ne soyons pas nés du même père, en attendant, prépare mon retour . . . Je sais que ma mère me pardonnera volontiers. Mais [j'ai peur du roi, notre vénérable aïeul,] j'ai peur d'Arkel, malgré toute sa bonté, [car j'ai déçu par ce mariage étrange, tous ses projets politiques, et je crains que la beauté de Mélisande n'excuse pas à ses yeux, si sages, ma folie.]

---

[1] Scene Two of the opera.

his wise eyes, will not excuse my folly.] But if he consents to welcome her as if she were his own daughter, on the third evening after you get this letter, light a lantern at the top of the tower that looks over the sea. I shall see it from the bridge of my ship. If not, I shall sail on and never return . . ." What do you say?

S'il consent néanmoins à l'acceuillir comme il acceuillerait sa propre fille, le troisième soir qui suivra cette lettre, allume une lampe au sommet de la tour qui regarde la mer. Je l'apercevrai du pont de notre navire; sinon j'irai plus loin et ne reviendrai plus . . ." Qu'en dites-vous?

ARKEL

I can say nothing. [He has done what he probably had to do. I am very old, but I have never yet seen clearly into my own being, even for an instant; how do you suppose I am to judge what others do? I am not far from the grave and I am not yet able to pass judgement on myself . . . One is always mistaken unless one closes one's eyes to forgive or to look more closely at one's own being. This may move us strangely, but that's all. He is more than ripe in years and like a child he has married a young girl he found beside a spring . . .] All this perhaps may move us strangely, because we only ever see the underside of fate, I mean the underside of our fate . . . Until now he has always followed my advice. I thought I would make him happy when I sent him to seek the hand of the princess Ursule. He could not be alone, and since the death of his wife it made him sad to be alone; this marriage would have put an end to long war and to longstanding hatred. He would not have it so. Let it be as he wishes. I have never stood in the way of destiny. He knows his own future better than I. Perhaps in this world nothing ever occurs without purpose.

Je n'en dis rien. [Il a fait ce qu'il devait probablement faire. Je suis très vieux et cependant je n'ai pas encore vu clair, un instant, en moi-même; comment voulez-vous que je juge ce que d'autres ont fait? Je ne suis pas loin du tombeau et je ne parviens pas à me juger moi-même . . . On se trompe toujours lorsqu'on ne ferme pas les yeux pour pardonner ou pour mieux regarder en soi-même. Cela nous semble étrange; et voilà tout. Il a passé l'âge mûr et il épouse, comme un enfant, une petite fille qu'il trouve près d'une source . . .] Cela peut nous paraître étrange, parce que nous ne voyons jamais que l'envers des destinées . . . l'envers même de la nôtre . . . Il avait toujours suivi mes conseils jusqu'ici; j'avais cru le rendre heureux en l'envoyant demander la main de la princesse Ursule . . . Il ne pouvait pas rester seul, et depuis la mort de sa femme il était triste d'être seul; et ce mariage allait mettre fin à de longues guerres et à de vieilles haines . . . Il ne l'a pas voulu ainsi. Qu'il en soit comme il l'a voulu: je ne me suis jamais mis en travers d'une destinée; et il sait mieux que moi son avenir. Il n'arrive peut-être pas d'événements inutiles . . .

GENEVIEVE

He was always so thoughtful, so serious and resolute . . . [If it was Pelléas, I would understand . . . But him . . . at his age . . . Who is he going to bring into our midst? An unknown girl found by the wayside . . .] Yet since the death of his wife he has lived only for his son, little Yniold. [If he intended to remarry it was because you wanted him to . . . And now . . . a young girl in the forest . . .] Everything else he neglects . . . what can we do?

Il a toujours été si prudent, si grave et si ferme . . . [Si c'était Pelléas, je comprendrais . . . Mais lui . . . à son âge . . . Qui va-t-il introduire ici? – Une inconnue trouvée le long des routes . . .] Depuis la mort de sa femme il ne vivait plus que pour son fils, le petit Yniold, [et s'il allait se remarier, c'était parce que vous l'aviez voulu . . . Et maintenant . . . une petite fille dans la forêt . . .] Il a tout oublié . . . – Qu'allons-nous faire? . . .

(Enter Pelléas.) [8]

ARKEL

Who's that? Who has come in?

Qui est-ce qui entre là?

GENEVIEVE

It's Pelléas. He has been weeping.

C'est Pelléas. Il a pleuré.

ARKEL

Is that you, Pelléas? Come closer into the light, so that I may see you.

Est-ce toi, Pelléas? – Viens un peu plus près que je te voie dans la lumière . . .

PELLEAS

Grandfather, I received at the same time as the letter from my brother, another letter.

Grand-père, j'ai reçu, en même temps que la lettre de mon frère, une autre lettre; une

A letter from my friend Marcellus. He is on the point of death and he has sent for me. [He wants to see me before he dies . . .

lettre de mon ami Marcellus . . . Il va mourir et il m'appelle. [Il voudrait me voir avant de mourir . . .

ARKEL

You wish to leave before your brother's return? Perhaps your friend is less ill than he thinks . . .

Tu voudrais partir avant le retour de ton frère? – Ton ami est peut-être moins malade qu'il ne le croit . . .

PELLEAS

His letter is so sad one can see death between the lines.] He says he knows exactly the day that death will come. And he says I could be there in time to see him, if I wish; he says I have no time to lose. [The journey is very long, and if I wait for Golaud's return, it may be too late . . .]

Sa lettre est si triste qu'on voit la mort entre les lignes . . .] Il dit qu'il sait exactement le jour où la mort doit venir . . . Il me dit que je puis arriver avant elle si je veux, mais qu'il n'y a plus de temps à perdre. [Le voyage est très long et si j'attends le retour de Golaud, il sera peut-être trop tard . . .]

ARKEL

It would be well to wait a little time, however. We have no notion yet how your brother's return may affect us. And besides, is your father not here, in this very castle, closer to death perhaps than your friend? Can you make a choice between your father and your friend?

Il faudrait attendre quelque temps cependant . . . Nous ne savons pas ce que [1]ce retour nous prépare. Et d'ailleurs ton père n'est-il pas ici, au-dessus de nous, plus malade peut-être que ton ami . . . Pourras-tu choisir entre le père et l'ami?

(He goes out.)

GENEVIEVE

See that the lantern is lit this evening, Pelléas.

Aie soin d'allumer la lampe dès ce soir, Pelléas . . .

(They go out separately.)

[2] **Scene Four.** *Before the castle.* [9] *Enter Geneviève and Mélisande.*

MELISANDE

The gardens seem enshrouded in night. And such forest all round the castle!

Il fait sombre dans les jardins. Et quelles forêts tout autour des palais! . . .

GENEVIEVE

Yes, I too was struck by that when I first came here. It astonishes everyone who comes here. There are places here where you never see the sun. But you quickly get used to it. It is now many years, very many years, it is now nearly forty years that I have lived here. Look over there, on the other side, you get the light from the sea.

Oui; cela m'étonnait aussi quand je suis arrivée ici, et cela étonne tout le monde. Il y a des endroits où l'on ne voit jamais le soleil. Mais l'on s'y fait si vite . . . Il y a longtemps . . . Il y a près de quarante ans que je vis ici . . . Regardez de l'autre côté, vous aurez la clarté de la mer . . .

MELISANDE

I hear a sound somewhere below us . . .

J'entends du bruit au-dessous de nous . . .

GENEVIEVE

Yes, that is someone coming up here . . . Ah, it's Pelléas . . . Perhaps he is tired after waiting for you so long.

Oui; c'est quelqu'un qui monte vers nous . . . Ah! c'est Pelléas . . . Il semble encore fatigué de vous avoir attendue si longtemps . . .

MELISANDE

He hasn't seen us.

Il ne nous a pas vues.

---

[1] le retour de son frère

[2] Scene Three of the opera.

I think he has, but doesn't know what he should do. Pelléas, Pelléas, is that you?

Je crois qu'il nous a vues, mais il ne sait ce qu'il doit faire . . . Pelléas, Pelléas, est-ce toi?

PELLEAS

Yes! I was going in search of the sea . . .

Oui! . . . Je venais du côté de la mer . . .

GENEVIEVE

So were we; we came here for the light. For here the light is brighter than elsewhere; and yet the sea is dark.

Nous aussi; nous cherchions la clarté. Ici, il fait un peu plus clair qu'ailleurs; et cependant la mer est sombre.

PELLEAS

A storm is gathering for tonight; there has been one every night for several days and yet the sea is very calm this evening . . . [10] One could easily put out to sea without knowing and never return.

Nous aurons une tempête cette nuit. Il y en a toutes les nuits depuis quelque temps . . . et cependant la mer est si calme ce soir . . . On s'embarquerait sans le savoir et l'on ne reviendrait plus.

[1]MELISANDE

Something's putting out to sea . . .

Quelque chose sort du port . . .

PELLEAS

It's an unusually large ship, for her lights are very high. We will see her any minute, as soon as she sails into the next patch of light . . .

Il faut que ce soit un grand navire . . . Les lumières sont très hautes, nous le verrons tout à l'heure quand il entrera dans la bande de clarté. . .

GENEVIEVE

I do not think we'll be able to see her. There is still a mist hanging over the sea.

Je ne sais si nous pourrons le voir . . . il y a encore une brume sur la mer . . .

PELLEAS

Soon perhaps the mist will slowly clear away . . .

On dirait que la brume s'élève lentement . . .

MELISANDE

Yes, down there in the distance I can see a faint light I had not seen before . . .

Oui; j'aperçois, là-bas, une petite lumière que je n'avais pas vue . . .

PELLEAS

It's a beacon; there are several others still out of sight in the mist.

C'est un phare; il y en a d'autres que nous ne voyons pas encore.

MELISANDE

Now the ship has moved into the light. She's already far out.

Le navire est dans la lumière . . . Il est déjà bien loin . . .

PELLEAS

[It's a foreign ship. It looks larger than ours . . .

[C'est un navire étranger. Il me semble plus grand que les nôtres . . .

MELISANDE

It's the ship that brought me here! . . .]

C'est le navire qui m'a menée ici! . . .]

PELLEAS

Under way, in full sail . . .

Il s'éloigne à toutes voiles . . .

MELISANDE

That is the ship that brought me here. The ship with big sails. I recognise her by her sails.

C'est le navire qui m'a menée ici. Il a de grandes voiles . . . Je le reconnais à ses voiles . . .

---

[1] **VOICES OFFSTAGE** Hoé! Hoé! Hissé hoé! [11]

She will have stormy weather tonight . . .   Il aura mauvaise mer cette nuit . . .

MELISANDE

Why set sail on such a rough night? She is   Pourquoi s'en va-t-il cette nuit? . . . On ne
almost out of sight. Perhaps she'll be   le voit presque plus . . . Il fera peut-être
shipwrecked!   naufrage . . .

PELLEAS

The night is falling fast.   La nuit tombe très vite . . .

[(*silence*)]

GENEVIEVE

[Is no one going to speak? Have you   [Personne ne parle plus? . . . Vous n'avez
nothing more to say?] It is time to go back.   plus rien à vous dire? . . .] Il est temps de
Pelléas, show Mélisande the way. I have to   rentrer. Pelléas, montre la route à Mélisande.
go and look after little Yniold.   Il faut que j'aille voir, un instant, le petit
     Yniold.

(*She goes out.*)

PELLEAS

Nothing more can be seen out there . . .   On ne voit plus rien sur la mer . . .

MELISANDE

I can see some other lights.   Je vois d'autres lumières.

PELLEAS

They are the other beacons. Can you hear   Ce sont les autres phares . . . Entendez-
the sea? The wind is getting up. We'll go   vous la mer? . . . C'est le vent qui s'élève . . .
down by this path. Shall I hold your hand?   Descendons par ici. Voulez-vous me donner
     la main?

MELISANDE

But look! You see my hands are holding   Voyez, voyez, j'ai les mains pleines.[1]
these flowers.

PELLEAS

I'll take you by the arm, the path is very [12]   Je vous soutiendrai par le bras, le chemin
steep, and it's dark all around now. I'm   est escarpé et il y fait très sombre . . . Je
leaving tomorrow maybe . . .   pars peut-être demain . . .

MELISANDE

Oh! . . .Why are you leaving?   Oh! . . .pourquoi partez-vous?

(*They go out.*) [13]

---

[1] pleines de fleurs.

Act Two

Scene One. *A well in the park. Enter Pelléas and Mélisande.* [14]

PELLEAS

I wonder if you know where I have brought you? I often come and sit here in the middle of the day, when it's too hot in the garden. Even under the trees today the air is stifling.

Vous ne savez pas où je vous ai menée? – Je viens souvent m'asseoir ici, vers midi, lorsqu'il fait trop chaud dans les jardins. On étouffe, aujourd'hui, même à l'ombre des arbres.

MELISANDE

Oh, what clear water . . .

[15] Oh! l'eau est claire . . .

PELLEAS

The water's clear and cool as winter. It's an old disused well. They say this was a well with miraculous powers. It would open the eyes of the blind. It is called to this day the Blind Man's Well.

Elle est fraiche comme l'hiver. C'est une vieille fontaine abandonnée. Il paraît que c'était une fontaine miraculeuse, – elle ouvrait les yeux des aveugles. – On l'appelle encore la "fontaine des aveugles".

MELISANDE

Does it no longer open the eyes of the blind?

Elle n'ouvre plus les yeux des aveugles?

PELLEAS

Since the king has become almost blind himself, no one comes here.

Depuis que le roi est presque aveugle lui-même, on n'y vient plus . . .

MELISANDE

How silent it is here, all alone . . .

Comme on est seul ici . . . On n'entend rien.

PELLEAS

This place is always unbelievably silent . . . One can hear the water sleeping. Would you like to sit here at the edge of the marble . . .? There is a linden tree where the sun never shines . . .

Il y a toujours un silence extraordinaire . . . On entendrait dormir l'eau . . . Voulez-vous vous asseoir au bord du bassin de marbre? Il y a un tilleul où le soleil n'entre jamais . . .

MELISANDE

Let me lie down on the marble. I want to see the bottom of the well . . .

Je vais me coucher sur le marbre. – Je voudrais voir le fond de l'eau . . .

PELLEAS

No one has ever seen it . . . Perhaps it is as deep as the sea. [No one knows where it comes from. It may come from the centre of the earth . . .]

On ne l'a jamais vu. – Elle est peut-être aussi profonde que la mer. [– On ne sait d'où elle vient. – Elle vient peut-être du fond de la terre . . .]

MELISANDE

If something bright were shining down there, perhaps one might see it . . .

Si quelque chose brillait au fond, on le verrait peut-être . . .

PELLEAS

Don't lean over like that.

[16] Ne vous penchez pas ainsi . . .

MELISANDE

I want to touch the water . . .

Je voudrais toucher l'eau . . .

49

PELLEAS

Take care not to slip . . . Let me hold your hand.

Prenez garde de glisser . . . Je vais vous tenir la main . . .

MELISANDE

No, no, I want to dip both my hands in . . . It's strange, my hands don't seem very well today . . .

Non, non, je voudrais y plonger mes deux mains . . . on dirait que mes mains sont malades aujourd'hui . . .

PELLEAS

Oh! Oh! Be careful. Do be careful. Mélisande! Mélisande! Oh! Look at your hair . . .

Oh! Oh! prenez garde! prenez garde! Mélisande! . . . Mélisande! . . . Oh! votre chevelure! . . .

MELISANDE
(sitting up)

I can't, I can't reach it.

Je ne peux pas, je ne peux pas l'atteindre.

PELLEAS

Your hair has fallen in the water . . .

Vos cheveux ont plongé dans l'eau . . .

MELISANDE

Yes. It's even longer than my arms . . . It's even longer than I am . . .

Oui, oui; ils sont plus longs que mes bras . . . Ils sont plus longs que moi . . .

[*(silence)*]

PELLEAS

Was it also by a spring that he found you?

C'est au bord d'une fontaine aussi, qu'il vous a trouvée?

MELISANDE

Yes . . .

Oui . . .

PELLEAS

What did he say?

Que vous a-t-il dit?

MELISANDE

Nothing. I don't remember . . .

Rien; – je ne me rappelle plus . . .

PELLEAS

Did he come close?

Etait-il tout près de vous?

MELISANDE

Yes, he wanted to kiss me . . .

Oui; il voulait m'embrasser . . .

PELLEAS

You didn't want him to?

Et vous ne vouliez pas?

MELISANDE

No.

Non.

PELLEAS

Why didn't you want him to?

Pourquoi ne vouliez-vous pas?

MELISANDE

Oh! Oh! I can see something moving at the bottom of the water . . .

Oh! oh! j'ai vu passer quelque chose au fond de l'eau . . .

PELLEAS

Be careful! Be careful! You'll fall in! What's that you're playing with?

Prenez garde! prenez garde! – Vous allez tomber! – Avec quoi jouez-vous?

MELISANDE

It's the ring he gave me.

[17] Avec l'anneau qu'il m'a donné . . .

[Take care, you'll lose it . . .

[Prenez garde; vous allez le perdre . . .

MELISANDE

No, no, my hands are quite safe . . .]

Non, non, je suis sûre de mes mains . . .]

PELLEAS

Don't play with it like that, not over such deep water . . .

Ne jouez pas ainsi, au-dessus d'une eau si profonde . . .

MELISANDE

You see, my hands are steady.

Mes mains ne tremblent pas.

PELLEAS

It sparkles in the sun. Don't throw it so high in the air.

Comme il brille au soleil! – Ne le jetez pas si haut vers le ciel . . .

MELISANDE

Oh!

Oh! . . .

PELLEAS

It's fallen in!

Il est tombé?

MELISANDE

It's fallen in the water!

Il est tombé dans l'eau! . . .

PELLEAS

Where is it? Where is it?

Où est-il?

MELISANDE

I didn't see it sinking.

Je ne le vois pas descendre . . .

PELLEAS

I think I can see it . . .

Je crois ¹que je la vois briller . . .

MELISANDE

My ring?

²Où donc?

PELLEAS

Yes, yes, down there . . .

Oui, oui; là-bas . . .

MELISANDE

Oh! Oh! It's so far away! . . . No, no, that's[18] not it, that's not my ring. My ring has gone . . . I've lost it! All it has left is a circle on the water . . . What are we going to do now?

Oh! oh! Elle est loin de nous! . . . non, non, ce n'est pas elle . . . ce n'est plus elle . . . Elle est perdue . . . perdue . . . Il n'y a plus qu'un grand cercle sur l'eau . . . Qu'allons-nous faire? Qu'allons-nous faire maintenant?

PELLEAS

There's no need to be distressed like this over a ring. It's nothing, perhaps we'll recover it. We might recover another one instead.

Il ne faut pas s'inquiéter ainsi pour une bague. Ce n'est rien . . . nous la retrouverons peut-être. Ou bien nous en trouverons une autre . . .

MELISANDE

No, no, we'll never recover it, we'll not find any other ones either . . . I thought I had it safely in my hands . . . I had already closed my hands. Even so it fell in . . . I threw it up too high, up into the sun.

Non, non; nous ne la retrouverons plus, nous n'en trouverons pas d'autres non plus . . . Je croyais l'avoir dans les mains cependant . . . J'avais déjà fermé les mains, et elle est tombée malgré tout . . . Je l'ai jetée trop haut, du côté du soleil . . .

---

¹ la voir briller . . .

² Ma bague?

Now come, we'll come back some other day. Come on, we must go. They'll be coming to find us. The clock struck twelve as the ring fell into the water . . .

Venez, venez, nous reviendrons un autre jour . . . venez, il est temps. On irait à notre rencontre . . . Midi sonnait au moment où l'anneau est tombé . . .

MELISANDE

What shall we tell Golaud if he asks where it is?

Qu'allons-nous dire à Golaud s'il demande où il est?

PELLEAS

The truth, the truth, [the truth] . . .

La vérité, la vérité, [la vérité] . . .

(*They go out.*)

Scene Two. *A room in the castle. Golaud is discovered lying on his bed; Mélisande is at the bedside.*

GOLAUD

Ah! ah! all is well, it's nothing serious. But I am unable to explain how this could have happened. I was hunting unconcerned in the forest. Suddenly my horse just bolted for no reason. Could it have seen something unusual? Just before, I'd heard the clock strike the twelve strokes of noon, when on the last stroke, it took sudden fright and ran like a blind idiot into a tree! [I heard nothing more.] I can remember no more after that. I fell down, and the horse must have fallen on top of me; my chest felt as though the whole forest had fallen on me. My heart felt as though it had broken in two. But my heart is robust. I'm sure it's nothing serious . . .

Ah! ah! tout va bien, cela ne sera rien. Mais je ne puis m'expliquer comment cela s'est passé. Je chassais tranquillement dans la forêt. Mon cheval s'est emporté tout à coup, sans raison. A-t-il vu quelque chose d'extraordinaire? . . . Je venais d'entendre sonner les douze coups de midi. Au douzième coup, il s'effraie subitement, et court, comme un aveugle fou, contre un arbre. [Je n'ai plus rien entendu.] Je ne sais plus ce qui est arrivé. Je suis tombé, et lui doit être tombé sur moi. Je croyais avoir toute la forêt sur la poitrine; je croyais que mon cœur était [1]écrasé. Mais mon cœur est solide. Il paraît que ce n'est rien . . .

MELISANDE

Shall I give you a drink of water?

Voulez-vous boire un peu d'eau?

GOLAUD

No thank you, I'm not thirsty.

Merci, merci, je n'ai pas soif.

MELISANDE

May I bring you another pillow? . . . There's a little spot of blood on this one.

Voulez-vous un autre oreiller? . . . Il y a une petite tache de sang sur celui-ci.

GOLAUD

No, there's no need to change it. [My mouth was bleeding just now. I may bleed again . . .]

Non, non; ce n'est pas la peine. [J'ai saigné de la bouche tout à l'heure. Je saignerai peut-être encore . . .]

MELISANDE

Are you sure? I hope you're not in pain.

Est-ce bien sûr? . . . Vous ne souffrez pas trop?

GOLAUD

No, no, this is not the first time. I am made of blood and iron. [They are not little children's bones round my heart, don't worry . . .]

Non, non, j'en ai vu bien d'autres. Je suis fait au fer et au sang . . . [Ce ne sont pas des petits os d'enfant que j'ai autour du cœur, ne t'inquiète pas . . .]

MELISANDE

Close your eyes and try to sleep. I shall be here beside you all night . . .

Fermez les yeux et tâchez de dormir. Je resterai ici toute la nuit . . .

[1] déchiré

GOLAUD

No, no, I don't want you to weary yourself in that way. There's nothing more I need. I shall sleep like a child. What is it, Mélisande? What brings these tears to your eyes?

Non, non; je ne veux pas que tu te fatigues ainsi. Je n'ai besoin de rien; je dormirai comme un enfant ... Qu'y a-t-il, Mélisande? Pourquoi pleures-tu tout à coup? ...

MÉLISANDE
(weeping)

I'm ... I'm not very well ...

Je suis ... Je suis malade aussi ...

GOLAUD

You're not well? What is it? What is it, Mélisande?

Tu es malade? ... Qu'as-tu donc, Mélisande? ...

MÉLISANDE [3]

I don't know ... I am not very well here. I would rather you knew today; my lord, I am not happy here.

Je ne sais pas ... Je suis malade ici ... Je préfère vous le dire aujourd'hui; seigneur, je ne suis pas heureuse ici ...

GOLAUD

But what can have happened? [Mélisande? What is it? I had no idea ... What's happened?] Has someone done you wrong? Has someone been offensive to you?

Qu'est-il donc arrivé, [Mélisande? Qu'est-ce que c'est? ... Moi qui ne me doutais de rien ... Qu'est-il donc arrivé? ...] Quelqu'un t'a fait du mal? ... Quelqu'un t'aurait offensée?

MÉLISANDE

No, no, no one has done me any wrong at all ... It's not that. [But I can't go on living here, I don't know why. I want to go away, go away! I'll die if I have to stay here ...

Non, non; personne ne m'a fait le moindre mal ... Ce n'est pas cela ... [Mais je ne puis plus vivre ici. Je ne sais pas pourquoi ... Je voudrais m'en aller, m'en aller! ... Je vais mourir si l'on me laisse ici ...

GOLAUD

Has something happened?] Then you must be concealing something from me. Tell me plainly, tell me the truth, Mélisande. Is it the king? Is it my mother? Is it Pelléas?

Mais il est arrivé quelque chose?] Tu dois me cacher quelque chose? ... Dis-moi toute la vérité, Mélisande ... Est-ce le roi? ... Est-ce ma mère? ... Est-ce Pelléas? ...

MÉLISANDE

No, no, it is not Pelléas. It isn't anyone ... You cannot understand me ...

Non, non, ce n'est pas Pelléas. Ce n'est personne ... Vous ne pouvez pas me comprendre ...

GOLAUD

[Why don't I understand? If you tell me nothing, how can I do anything for you? Tell me everything, then I'll understand.

[Pourquoi ne comprendrais-je pas? ... Si tu ne me dis rien, que veux-tu que je fasse ... Dis-moi tout, et je comprendrai tout.

MÉLISANDE

I don't know what it is myself. If I could tell you I would ...] It is something stronger than I ...

Je ne sais pas moi-même ce que c'est ... Si je pouvais vous le dire, je vous le dirais ...] C'est quelque chose qui est plus fort que moi ...

GOLAUD

Come, let us be reasonable, Mélisande. What do you want me to do? You are no longer a child. – Is it me you would like to be rid of?

Voyons; sois raisonnable, Mélisande. –Que veux-tu que je fasse? – Tu n'es plus une enfant. – Est-ce moi que tu voudrais quitter?

Oh no, it's not that. I would like to go away with you. It's here that I can't live any longer . . . I feel that I will not live much longer . . .

Oh! non, non; ce n'est pas cela . . . Je voudrais m'en aller avec vous . . . C'est ici, que je ne peux plus vivre . . . Je sens que je ne [1]vivrai plus longtemps . . .

GOLAUD

But there must be a reason for it. It will seem an act of madness. They will think it is all childish dreams. Let's see, is it Pelléas perhaps? I have not seen him speaking to you much.

Mais il faut une raison cependant. On va te croire folle. On va croire à des rêves d'enfant. – Voyons, est-ce Pelléas, peut-être? – Je crois qu'il ne te parle pas souvent . . .

MELISANDE

Yes, he speaks to me sometimes. I don't believe he likes me; I can see by his eyes . . . But he speaks to me whenever he sees me . . .

Si, si; il me parle parfois. Il ne m'aime pas, je crois; je l'ai vu dans ses yeux . . . Mais il me parle quand il me rencontre . . .

GOLAUD

You must not take offence at that. He has always been like that. He is rather unusual. [And at the moment he is sad; he is concerned for his friend Marcellus who is on the point of death and whom he cannot visit . . .] He will change, you'll see. He is young still . . .

Il ne faut pas lui en vouloir. Il a toujours été ainsi. Il est un peu étrange. [Et maintenant, il est triste; il songe à son ami Marcellus, qui est sur le point de mourir et qu'il ne peut pas aller voir . . .] Il changera, il changera, tu verras; il est jeune . . .

MELISANDE

But it's not that . . . it's not that . . .

Mais ce n'est pas cela . . . ce n'est pas cela . . .

GOLAUD

Then what is it? Can you not live the kind of life that we lead here? Is it too desolate here? It is true that the castle is ancient and gloomy. It is very cold and dark, and the people who live here are already old. And the country can seem desolate too, with these forests all around, all these ancient forests closed to the daylight. But all this could be brighter if anyone wants. And yet contentment, contentment . . . One cannot have that every day. [One must take things as they are.] But come, tell me something; no matter what; I will do whatever you wish . . .

Qu'est-ce donc? Ne peux-tu pas te faire à la vie qu'on mène ici? – Fait-il trop triste ici? – Il est vrai que ce château est très vieux et très sombre . . . Il est très froid et très profond. Et tous ceux qui l'habitent sont déjà vieux. Et la campagne semble bien triste aussi, avec toutes [2]ses forêts, toutes [2]ses vieilles forêts sans lumière. Mais on peut égayer tout cela si l'on veut. Et puis, la joie, on n'en a pas tous les jours; [il faut prendre les choses comme elles sont.] Mais dis-moi quelque chose; n'importe quoi; je ferai tout ce que tu voudras . . .

MELISANDE

Yes, it's true. No one ever sees the daylight here. I saw it for the first time today.

Oui, oui; c'est vrai . . . on ne voit jamais le ciel ici . . . Je l'ai vu pour la première fois ce matin . . .

GOLAUD

Can it be that that makes you weep, my poor Mélisande? Is it just that? You weep because you never see the sky? Come, come, you're too old to weep about a thing like that. Do you think the summer will never come? You will see the sky every day. And then next year . . . Come, come, give me your hand; give me both your little hands.

C'est donc cela qui te fait pleurer, ma pauvre Mélisande? – Ce n'est donc que cela? – Tu pleures de ne pas voir le ciel? – Voyons, voyons, tu n'es plus à l'âge où l'on peut pleurer pour ces choses . . . Et puis l'été n'est-il pas là? Tu vas voir le ciel tous les jours. – Et puis l'année prochaine . . . Voyons, donne-moi ta main; donne-moi tes deux petites mains.

[1] vivrais
[2] ces

(He takes her hands.)

Oh! What little hands! I could crush them just as if they were flowers . . . Look! Why is the ring that I gave you not there?

Oh! ces petites mains que je pourrais écraser comme des fleurs . . . – Tiens, où est l'anneau que je t'avais donné?

MELISANDE

The ring?

L'anneau?

GOLAUD

Yes, your wedding ring. Where is it?

Oui; la bague de nos noces, où est-elle?

MELISANDE

I think . . . it must have fallen off . . .

Je crois . . . Je crois qu'elle est tombée . . .

GOLAUD

Fallen off? Where can it have fallen? I hope you haven't lost it?

Tombée? – Où est-elle tombée? – Tu ne l'as pas perdue?

MELISANDE

No, it has fallen off . . . It must have fallen off, but I know where it is . . .

Non, non; elle est tombée . . . elle doit être tombée . . . mais je sais où elle est . . .

GOLAUD

Where is it?

Où est-elle?

MELISANDE

You know the place . . . You know the place . . . You know the cave by the sea?

Vous savez . . . vous savez bien . . . la grotte au bord de la mer?

GOLAUD

Yes.

Oui.

MELISANDE

It's there, it's there, it must be there . . . Yes, yes, now I remember. I went down there this morning to gather up some sea-shells for little Yniold. There are some lovely ones there . . . It slipped from my finger . . . but the tide was rising, so I had to go before I was able to find it.

Eh bien, c'est là . . . Il faut que ce soit là . . . Oui, oui; je me rappelle . . . J'y suis allée ce matin, ramasser des coquillages pour le petit Yniold . . . Il y en a de très beaux . . . Elle a glissé de mon doigt . . . puis la mer est entrée; et j'ai dû sortir avant de l'avoir retrouvée.

GOLAUD

Are you certain it is there?

Es-tu sûre que ce soit là?

MELISANDE

Yes, yes, I am certain . . . I felt it slip off . . . [Then suddenly, the sound of the waves . . .]

Oui, oui; tout à fait sûre . . . Je l'ai sentie glisser . . . [puis tout à coup, le bruit des vagues . . .]

GOLAUD

You will have to go and find it immediately.

Il faut aller la chercher tout de suite.

MELISANDE

Go there now? Immediately? In the dark?

Maintenant? – tout de suite? – dans l'obscurité?

GOLAUD

Go there now, immediately, in the dark! I would prefer to lose everything I possess rather than lose that ring. You do not know what it is. You do not know where it came from. It will be a high tide tonight. The sea will probably get there before you, you must be quick. [You must go and look for it at once . . .]

Maintenant, tout de suite, dans l'obscurité . . . J'aimerais mieux avoir perdu tout ce que j'ai plutôt que d'avoir perdu cette bague. Tu ne sais pas ce que c'est. Tu ne sais pas d'où elle vient. La mer sera très haute cette nuit. La mer viendra la prendre avant toi . . . dépêche-toi. [Il faut aller la chercher tout de suite . . .]

MELISANDE

I'm afraid ... I'm afraid to go alone there ...

Je n'ose pas ... Je n'ose pas aller seule ...

GOLAUD

Go now! Take someone if you like, but go! So long as you go this moment, understand? You must be quick. Go and see if Pelléas will go with you.

Vas-y, vas-y avec n'importe qui. Mais il faut y aller tout de suite, entends-tu? – Dépêche-toi; demande à Pelléas d'y aller avec toi.

MELISANDE

Pelléas? Go with Pelléas? But Pelléas won't want to go.

Pelléas? – Avec Pelléas? – Mais Pelléas ne voudra pas ...

GOLAUD

Pelléas will do anything you ask him. I know Pelléas better than you. But go, go at once. I shall not sleep until I have the ring back.

Pelléas fera tout ce que tu lui demandes. Je connais Pelléas mieux que toi. Vas-y, vas-y, hâte-toi. Je ne dormirai pas avant d'avoir la bague.

MELISANDE

Oh, oh! I'm so unhappy, I'm so unhappy ...

Je ne suis pas heureuse! ...

(She goes out weeping.)

Scene Three. *Before a cave. Enter Pelléas and Mélisande.*

PELLEAS
(speaking with great agitation)

Yes, this is it, we are here. It's so dark that the entrance to the cave is indistinguishable from the night. There are no stars to be seen in the sky. If we wait till the moon has broken through the clouds it will shed light far into the cave and then we can enter in safety. There are dangerous places along here for the path is very narrow and it winds between two lakes of unfathomable depth. I never remembered, we should have brought a torch with us, or a lantern. But perhaps we can see by the light of the sky. Have you never been into this cave before?

Oui; c'est ici, nous y sommes. Il fait si noir que l'entrée de la grotte ne se distingue pas du reste de la nuit ... Il n'y a pas d'étoiles de ce côté. Attendons que la lune ait déchiré ce grand nuage; elle éclairera toute la grotte et alors nous pourrons y entrer sans danger. Il y a des endroits dangereux et le sentier est très étroit, entre deux lacs dont on n'a pas encore trouvé le fond. Je n'ai pas songé à emporter une torche ou une lanterne, mais je pense que la clarté du ciel nous suffira. – Vous n'avez jamais pénétré dans cette grotte?

MELISANDE

No ...

Non ...

PELLEAS

Let's go in ... You must be able to describe the place where you lost the ring in case he should ask you. It is both large and beautiful. [There are stalactites which look like plants, or men.] It is full of deep blue shadows. [No one has yet explored it right through. There is supposed to be hidden treasure here. You'll see wreckage from old shipwrecks. You must not attempt it without a guide. Some have been in and never come back. I don't dare go too far in myself. We'll stop the moment we can no longer see the light of the sea or the sky.] If you light a candle inside the cave it is as though the roof were covered with stars, as if it were the sky. [They are said to be fragments of crystal and salt glittering in the rock. Look, look! I feel the heavens will open ...] Let me hold your hand. [Don't be afraid!] You needn't be afraid, there's no danger at all.

Entrons-y ... Il faut pouvoir décrire l'endroit où vous avez perdu la bague, s'il vous interroge ... Elle est très grande et très belle. [Il y a des stalactites qui ressemblent à des plantes et à des hommes.] Elle est pleine de ténèbres bleues. [On ne l'a pas encore explorée jusqu'au fond. On y a, paraît-il, caché de grands trésors. Vous y verrez les épaves d'anciens naufrages. Mais il ne faut pas s'y engager sans guide. Il en est qui ne sont jamais revenus. Moi-même je n'ose pas aller trop avant. Nous nous arrêterons au moment où nous n'apercevrons plus la clarté de la mer ou du ciel.] Quand on y allume une petite lumière, on dirait que la voûte est couverte d'étoiles, comme le ciel. [Ce sont, dit-on, des fragments de cristal ou de sel qui brillent ainsi dans le rocher. – Voyez, voyez, je crois que le ciel va s'ouvrir ...] Donnez-moi la main,

We'll go no further the moment we no longer see the light of the sea. Is it the noise of the cave you are afraid of? [It's the noise of the night or the noise of the silence . . .] Listen, can you hear the sea behind us? It seems to be unhappy tonight. Oh! Here is the light!

ne tremblez pas, ne tremblez pas ainsi. Il n'y a pas de danger: nous nous arrêterons au moment où nous n'apercevrons plus la clarté de la mer . . . Est-ce le bruit de la grotte qui vous effraie? [C'est le bruit de la nuit ou le bruit du silence . . .] Entendez-vous la mer derrière nous? – Elle ne semble pas heureuse cette nuit . . . Ah! voici la clarté!

(*The moon throws a flood of light into the entrance and the interior of the cave, and reveals three white-haired beggars sitting side by side and holding one another up as they sleep leaning against a boulder.*) [19]

MELISANDE

Ah!   Ah!

PELLEAS

What is it?   [20] Qu'y a-t-il?

MELISANDE

Over there . . . Over there . . .   Il y a . . . Il y a . . .
(*She points to the three beggars.*)

PELLEAS

Yes, I can see them too . . .   Oui, oui; je les ai vus aussi . . .

MELISANDE

Let's go out! Let's go out!   Allons-nous-en! . . . Allons-nous-en! . . .

PELLEAS

They are three old beggars who have fallen asleep . . . There's a famine in the land . . . Why have they come here to sleep?

[Oui . . .] Ce sont trois vieux pauvres qui se sont endormis . . . Il y a une grande famine dans le pays . . . Pourquoi sont-ils venus dormir ici? . . .

MELISANDE

Let's go out; come . . . Let's go out!   Allons-nous-en! . . . Venez[, venez] . . . Allons-nous-en! . . .

PELLEAS

Be careful, don't speak so loudly . . . We must not wake them up . . . They are still sound asleep. Come on.

Prenez garde, ne parlez pas si haut . . . Ne les éveillons pas . . . Ils dorment encore profondément . . . Venez.

MELISANDE

Let me be; I would rather go alone . . .   Laissez-moi[, laissez-moi]; je préfère marcher seule . . .

PELLEAS

We'll come back some other day . . .   Nous reviendrons un autre jour . . .

(*They go out.*)

[1] [**Scene Four.** *A room in the castle. Arkel and Pelléas are discovered.*

ARKEL

So you see everything conspires to keep you here and prevent this pointless journey. Your father's condition has been kept from you until today, but he may have no hope. That alone should arrest your going. But there are so many other reasons. At a time when our foes are aroused, and the people

Vous voyez que tout vous retient ici et que tout vous interdit ce voyage inutile. On vous a caché jusqu'à ce jour, l'état de votre père; mais il est peut-être sans espoir; et cela seul devrait suffir à vous arrêter sur le seuil. Mais il y a tant d'autres raisons . . . Et ce n'est pas à l'heure où nos ennemis se

---

[1] This whole scene is omitted from the opera.

are dying of starvation and there is murmuring all around us, you have no right to desert us. And why this journey? Marcellus is dead. Life has more important obligations than a visit to a grave. You say you are tired of your inactive life; but if activity and duty are to be found by the wayside, you would probably pass them by in your haste to travel on. It would be better to await them at the gate and bid them enter the moment they pass. And they pass by dead. Have you never seen them? I hardly see them any more myself, but I can teach you to see them, and I'll show them to you any day you wish to call them. But listen to me: if you believe this journey is required of you by your innermost self I will not forbid you to undertake it, since you must know better than I what actions you need to offer your being or your destiny. I would simply ask you to wait until we know what will happen . . .

réveillent et où le peuple meurt de faim et murmure autour de nous que vous avez le droit de nous abandonner. Et pourquoi ce voyage? Marcellus est mort; et la vie a des devoirs plus graves que la visite d'un tombeau. Vous êtes las, dites-vous, de votre vie inactive; mais si l'activité et le devoir se trouvent sur les routes, on les reconnaît rarement dans la hâte du voyage. Il vaut mieux les attendre sur le seuil et les faire entrer au moment où ils passent; et ils passent tous les jours. Vous ne les avez jamais vus? Je n'y vois presque plus moi-même, mais je vous apprendrai à voir; et vous les montrerai le jour où vous voudrez leur faire signe. Mais cependant, écoutez-moi: si vous croyez que c'est du fond de votre vie que ce voyage est exigé, je ne vous interdis pas de l'entreprendre, car vous devez savoir, mieux que moi, les événements que vous devez offrir à votre être ou à votre destinée. Je vous demanderais seulement d'attendre que nous sachions ce qui doit arriver avant peu . . .

PELLEAS

How long must I wait?

Combien de temps faudra-t-il attendre?

ARKEL

A few weeks; perhaps a few days.

Quelques semaines; peut-être quelques jours. . .

PELLEAS

I'll wait . . .]

J'attendrai . . .]

Irène Joachim at the Opéra-Comique

Edward Johnson as Pelléas at the first performance at the Met.

Act Three

[¹**Scene One.** *A room in the castle. Pelléas and Mélisande are discovered. Mélisande is spinning with a distaff at the back of the room.*

PELLEAS

Yniold is not yet back. Where did he go?

Yniold ne revient pas; où est-il allé?

MELISANDE

He heard a noise in the passage. He went to see what it was.

Il avait entendu quelque bruit dans le corridor; il est allé voir ce que c'est.

PELLEAS

Mélisande . . .

Mélisande . . .

MELISANDE

What is it?

Qu'y a-t-il?

PELLEAS

Can you see to work by over there?

Y voyez-vous encore pour travailler? . . .

MELISANDE

I can work just as well in poor light . . .

Je travaille aussi bien dans l'obscurité . . .

PELLEAS

I think everyone in the castle's asleep. Golaud is not back from hunting. But it's late. Has he recovered from his fall?

Je crois que tout le monde dort déjà dans le château. Golaud ne revient pas de la chasse. Cependant il est tard . . . Il ne souffre plus de sa chute? . . .

MELISANDE

He said he had recovered.

Il a dit qu'il ne souffrait plus.

PELLEAS

He should take more care; he no longer has the supple body of a twenty-year-old . . . I can see stars through the window and moonlight on the trees. It's late. He won't be back.

Il devrait être plus prudent; il n'a plus le corps souple comme à vingt ans . . . Je vois les étoiles par la fenêtre et la clarté de la lune sur les arbres. Il est tard; il ne reviendra plus.

(*There is a knock at the door.*)

Who's there? . . . Come in! . . .

Qui est là? . . . Entrez! . . .

(*The door opens and little Yniold enters.*)

Was it you knocking like that? You shouldn't knock on doors like that, as if there were bad news. Look, you've frightened Mama.

C'est toi qui frappes ainsi? . . . Ce n'est pas ainsi qu'on frappe aux portes. C'est comme si un malheur venait d'arriver; regarde, tu as effrayé petite-mère.

YNIOLD

I only knocked very lightly . . .

Je n'ai frappé qu'un tout petit coup . . .

PELLEAS

It's late. Papa won't be back tonight. It's time you went to bed.

Il est tard; petit-père ne reviendra plus ce soir; il est temps de t'aller coucher.

YNIOLD

I won't go to bed before you.

Je n'irai pas me coucher avant vous.

---

¹ This whole scene is omitted from the opera.

59

PELLEAS

What? What did you say?	Quoi? . . . Qu'est-ce que tu dis là?

YNIOLD

I said . . . not before you go, not before you go . . .	Je dis . . . pas avant vous . . . pas avant vous . . .

(*He bursts into tears and runs for comfort to Mélisande.*)

MÉLISANDE

What is it, Yniold? What is it? Why burst into tears?	Qu'y a-t-il, Yniold? Qu'y a-t-il? . . . pourquoi pleures-tu tout à coup?

YNIOLD
(*sobbing*)

Because . . . Oh, oh! Because . . .	Parce que . . . Oh! oh! parce que . . .

MÉLISANDE

Why? . . . Why? . . . Tell me.	Pourquoi? . . . Pourquoi? . . . dis-le moi.

YNIOLD

Mama . . . Mama . . . You're going away . . .	Petite-mère . . . petite-mère . . . vous allez partir . . .

MÉLISANDE

What's got into you, Yniold? . . . I've never even thought of going away . . .	Mais qu'est-ce qui te prend, Yniold? . . . Je n'ai jamais songé à partir . . .

YNIOLD

Yes, yes! Papa's gone. Papa's not coming back, and you're going too. I can tell . . . I can tell . . .	Si, si; petit-père est parti . . . petit-père ne revient pas, et vous allez partir aussi . . . Je l'ai vu . . . je l'ai vu . . .

MÉLISANDE

But there's never been any question of it, Yniold . . . How can you tell I'm going?	Mais il n'a jamais été question de cela, Yniold . . . A quoi donc as-tu vu que j'allais partir?

YNIOLD

I can tell . . . I can tell . . . You told my uncle things I couldn't hear . . .	Je l'ai vu . . . je l'ai vu . . . Vous avez dit à mon oncle des choses que je ne pouvais pas entendre . . .

PELLEAS

He's sleepy, he's dreaming. Come here, Yniold. Are you sleepy already? . . . Come and look out of the window; the swans are fighting the dogs. . . .	Il a sommeil . . . il a rêvé . . . Viens ici, Yniold; tu dors déjà? . . . Viens donc voir à la fenêtre; les cygnes se battent contre les chiens . . .

YNIOLD
(*at the window*)

Oh, oh! They're chasing the dogs! They're chasing them! Oh, oh! The water! Their wings, their wings! They're frightened . . .	Oh! oh! Ils les chassent, les chiens! . . . Ils les chassent! . . . Oh! oh! l'eau! . . . les ailes! . . . les ailes! . . . Ils ont peur . . .

PELLEAS
(*going over to Mélisande*)

He's sleepy; he's fighting his sleepiness and his eyes are closing . . .	Il a sommeil; il lutte contre le sommeil et ses yeux se ferment . . .

MÉLISANDE
(*singing quietly as she spins*)

St Daniel and St Michael . . . St Michael and St Raphael . . .	Saint Daniel et Saint Michel . . . Saint Michel et Saint Raphaël . . .

60

(at the window)

Oh, oh! Mama! . . .   Oh! oh! petite-mère! . . .

MELISANDE
(rising brusquely)

What is it, Yniold? What is it?   Qu'y a-t-il, Yniold? . . . Qu'y a-t-il? . . .

YNIOLD

I've seen something out of the window . . .   J'ai vu quelque chose à la fenêtre . . .

(Pelléas and Mélisande run to the window.)

PELLEAS

It's nothing. I can see nothing . . .   Mais il n'y a rien. Je ne vois rien . . .

MELISANDE

Nor can I . . .   Moi non plus . . .

PELLEAS

Where did you see something? Which side?   Où as-tu vu quelque chose? De quel côté?

YNIOLD

There, over there! It's gone . . .   Là-bas, là-bas! . . . Elle n'y est plus . . .

PELLEAS

He doesn't know what he's saying. He   Il ne sait plus ce qu'il dit. Il aura vu la clarté
must have seen the moonlight on the   de la lune sur la forêt. Il y a souvent
forest. You often get unusual reflections.   d'étranges reflets . . . ou bien quelque chose
Or perhaps something went along the road   aura passé sur la route . . . ou dans son
. . . or in his sleep. Look, you see! I think   sommeil. Car voyez, voyez, je crois qu'il
he's sound asleep.   s'endort tout à fait . . .

YNIOLD
(at the window)

Papa's there! Papa's there!   Petit-père est là! petit-père est là!

PELLEAS
(going to the window)

He's right! That's Golaud coming into the   Il a raison: Golaud entre dans la cour . . .
courtyard . . .

YNIOLD

Papa! Papa! I'll go and meet him!   Petit-père! . . . petit-père! . . . Je vais à sa
                                       rencontre! . . .

(He runs out. A silence follows.)

PELLEAS

They're coming upstairs. . .   Ils montent l'escalier . . .

(Enter Golaud and little Yniold carrying a lamp.)

GOLAUD

Are you still waiting, in the dark?   Vous attendez encore dans l'obscurité?

YNIOLD

I've brought a lamp, Mama, a big lamp!   J'ai apporté une lumière, petite-mère, une
                                       grande lumière! . . .

(He raises the lamp and looks at Mélisande.)

Were you crying, Mama? Were you crying?   Tu as pleuré, petite-mère? Tu as pleuré? . . .

(He lifts the lamp towards Pelléas and looks at him too.)

You too, were you crying? Papa! Look,   Vous aussi, vous avez pleuré? . . . Petit-
papa! They've both been crying . . .   père, regarde, petit-père; ils ont pleuré tous
                                       les deux . . .

Don't hold the lamp in their eyes like that . . .]	Ne leur mets pas ainsi la lumière sous les yeux . . .]

¹**Scene Two.** *One of the towers of the castle. A watchman's path passes under one of the windows of the tower.*

MELISANDE
(at the window, combing her hair)

My hair's so long It reaches to the foot of the tower: My hair is waiting for you All the way down the tower . . . It waits for you all day, It waits for you all day.	[21] Mes longs cheveux descendent Jusqu'au seuil de la tour; Mes cheveux vous attendent Tout le long de la tour, - Et tout le long du jour, Et tout le long du jour.
St Daniel and St Michael, St Michael and St Raphael, I was born on a Sunday, On a Sunday at noon . . .	Saint Daniel et Saint Michel, Saint Michel et Saint Raphaël, Je suis née un dimanche, Un dimanche à midi . . .

(Pelléas enters by the path.)

PELLEAS

Holà! Holà! Ho!	Holà! Holà! Ho!

MELISANDE

Who's there?	Qui est là?

PELLEAS

Me, me, and me! . . . What are you doing at the window, singing like some rare exotic bird?	Moi, moi, et moi! . . . Que fais-tu là à la fenêtre en chantant comme un oiseau qui n'est pas d'ici?

MELISANDE

I'm undoing my hair for the night . . .	J'arrange mes cheveux pour la nuit . . .

PELLEAS

Is that what I can see there against the wall? I thought it was a light you had in there . . .	C'est là ce que je vois sur le mur? . . . Je croyais que tu avais de la lumière . . .

MELISANDE

I have opened the window. I was too warm in the tower. It's such a beautiful night . . .	J'ai ouvert la fenêtre; il fait trop chaud dans la tour . . . il fait beau cette nuit . . .

PELLEAS

There's a myriad of stars in the heavens; I've never seen so many stars before . . . But the moon is still over the sea . . . Come forward out of the shadow, Mélisande, lean out of the window, so that I can see your hair falling loose.	Il y a d'innombrables étoiles; je n'en ai jamais autant vu que ce soir; . . . mais la lune est encore sur la mer . . . Ne reste pas dans l'ombre, Mélisande, penche-toi un peu, que je voie tes cheveux dénoués.

MELISANDE
(Mélisande leans out of the window.)

I look so plain like this . . .	Je suis affreuse ainsi . . .

PELLEAS

Oh! Mélisande . . . Oh! you are beautiful! Beautiful like that! Lean out! Yes, lean out! Let me come a little nearer to you.	Oh! Mélisande! . . . oh! tu es belle! . . . tu es belle ainsi! . . . penche-toi! penche-toi! . . . laisse-moi venir plus près de toi . . .

¹ Scene One of the opera. Maeterlinck substituted a different song in later editions of the play.

MELISANDE

I cannot reach down any nearer to you . . .
I'm leaning out as far as I can . . .

Je ne puis pas venir plus près . . . je me
penche tant que je peux . . .

PELLEAS

I cannot climb any higher . . . Let me hold
your hand at least tonight before I go away.
I'm leaving tomorrow.

Je ne puis pas monter plus haut . . . donne-
moi du moins ta main ce soir . . . avant que
je m'en aille . . . Je pars demain . . .

MELISANDE

No, no, no!

Non, non, non . . .

PELLEAS

Yes, yes, I must. Tomorrow I must go . . .
Let me touch your hand, your hand, let me
touch your hand with my lips . . .

Si, si; je pars, je partirai demain . . . donne-
moi ta main, ta petite main sur mes
lèvres . . .

MELISANDE

I shall not let you touch my hand if you
go . . .

Je ne te donne pas ma main si tu pars . . .

PELLEAS

Let me, let me, let me . . .

Donne, donne . . .

MELISANDE

Then you promise to stay?

Tu ne partiras pas?

PELLEAS

I shall wait, I shall wait . . .

J'attendrai, j'attendrai . . .

MELISANDE

I can see a rose down there in the darkness . . .

Je vois une rose dans les ténèbres . . .

PELLEAS

A rose? I can see nothing but the willow
hanging over the wall . . .

Où donc? . . . Je ne vois que les branches
du saule qui [1]dépassent le mur . . .

MELISANDE

Further down, further down in the garden,
over there where the shadow's dark and
green . . .

Plus bas, plus bas, dans le jardin; là-bas,
dans le vert sombre.

PELLEAS

But that's not a rose there . . . I will look in a
moment, but give me your hand first; first
your hand . . .

Ce n'est pas une rose . . . J'irai voir tout à
l'heure, mais donne-moi ta main d'abord;
d'abord ta main . . .

MELISANDE

There you are . . . there you are. I can't lean
out any further.

Voilà, voilà; . . . je ne puis me pencher
davantage . . .

PELLEAS

Lean further! I still can't reach your hand
with my lips.

Mes lèvres ne peuvent pas atteindre ta
main . . .

MELISANDE

I can't lean out any further . . . If I lean any
further I'll fall . . . Oh! oh! Look, my hair
has fallen down.

Je ne puis pas me pencher davantage . . . Je
suis sur le point de tomber . . . – Oh! oh!
mes cheveux descendent de la tour! . . .

(*As she leans her hair suddenly unwinds and envelops Pelléas.*)

---

[1] dépasse

Oh! Oh! What's this? Your hair, your hair has fallen over me! All your hair, Mélisande, all your hair has come down, all your hair has come down. In my hands, in my mouth . . . I run your hair through my fingers. Then I hold it in my arms, then I let it fall round my neck . . . I shall not open my hands again tonight.

Oh! oh! qu'est-ce que c'est? . . . Tes cheveux, tes cheveux descendent vers moi! . . . Toute ta chevelure, Mélisande, toute ta chevelure est tombée de la tour! . . . Je les tiens dans les mains, je les tiens dans la bouche . . . Je les tiens dans les bras, je les mets autour de mon cou . . . Je n'ouvrirai plus les mains cette nuit . . .

MELISANDE

Let me go! Let me go! If you don't I might fall!

Laisse-moi! laisse-moi! . . . Tu vas me faire tomber! . . .

PELLEAS

No, no, no! Never in my life have I seen hair like yours, Mélisande! Look, look, look, it comes from so high up and falls so far it envelops my very heart. It falls down so low it envelops my knees. And it is soft, soft as if it had fallen from heaven . . . and now heaven is hidden from me by your hair. Look, look. My two hands are not enough to hold it all; some of it even reaches the branch of the willow . . . In my hands it comes alive as if it were a bird, and it loves me, it loves me more than you!

Non, non, non; . . . je n'ai jamais vu de cheveux comme les tiens, Mélisande! . . . Vois, vois; ils viennent de si haut et m'inondent jusqu'au coeur . . . Ils m'inondent encore jusqu'aux genoux! . . . Et ils sont doux, ils sont doux comme ils tombaient du ciel! . . . Je ne vois plus le ciel à travers tes cheveux. Tu vois, tu vois? . . . mes deux mains ne peuvent pas les tenir; il y en a jusque sur les branches du saule . . . Ils vivent comme des oiseaux dans mes mains, ils m'aiment, ils m'aiment plus que toi! . . .

MELISANDE

Let me go, let me go . . . someone might come . . .

Laisse-moi, laisse-moi . . . quelqu'un pourrait venir . . .

PELLEAS

No, no, no, I shall not give you your freedom tonight. You are my prisoner tonight, all night long, all night long . . .

Non, non, non; je ne te délivre pas cette nuit . . . Tu es ma prisonnière cette nuit; toute la nuit, toute la nuit . . .

MELISANDE

Pelléas! Pelléas!

Pelléas! Pelléas! . . .

PELLEAS

I will tie your hair to the branch of the [22] willow. You will never go free, you will never go free. Look! Look! I want to kiss your hair . . . I don't suffer any more when I'm lost in your hair . . . Can you hear my kisses travelling along your hair? My kisses flow up along your hair. Each strand of your hair carries kisses. You see, you see, I can open my hands . . . My hands are free, but you cannot tear yourself away . . .

Je les noue, je les noue aux branches du saule . . . Tu ne t'en iras plus . . . tu ne t'en iras plus . . . Regarde, regarde, j'embrasse tes cheveux . . . Je ne souffre plus au milieu de tes cheveux . . . Tu entends mes baisers le long de tes cheveux . . . Il faut que chacun t'en apporte . . . Tu vois, tu vois, je puis ouvrir les mains . . . Tu vois, j'ai les mains libres et tu ne peux m'abandonner . . .

(*Some doves come out of the tower and fly about them in the darkness.*)

MELISANDE

Oh! Oh! You've hurt me! What is that, Pelléas? What is that flying above me?

Oh oh! tu m'as fait mal! Qu'y a-t-il, Pelléas? – Qu'est-ce qui vole autour de moi?

PELLEAS

Those are the doves that live in the tower . . . I must have frightened them. Now they have flown away.

Ce sont les colombes qui sortent de la tour . . . Je les ai effrayées; elles s'envolent . . .

Those are my doves, Pelléas. Leave me now, let's go. They will never come back . . .

Ce sont mes colombes, Pelléas. – Allons-nous-en, laisse-moi; elles ne reviendraient plus . . .

PELLEAS

Tell me, why will they never come back?

Pourquoi ne reviendraient-elles plus?

MÉLISANDE

They are sure to get lost in the darkness. Let me go! Let me hold up my head . . . I hear footsteps . . . Let me go! It's Golaud . . . I think it's Golaud! He must have heard us . . .

Elles se perdront dans l'obscurité . . . Laisse-moi relever la tête . . . J'entends un bruit de pas . . . Laisse-moi! – C'est Golaud! . . . Je crois que c'est Golaud! . . . Il nous a entendus . . .

PELLEAS

Stay still! Stay still! Your hair is caught in the tree. It's caught in the branches in the dark. Stay still! Stay still! It's dark now . . .

Attends! Attends! . . . Tes cheveux sont autour des branches . . . Ils se sont accrochés dans l'obscurité . . . Attends, attends! . . . Il fait noir . . .

(*Golaud enters by the path.*) [23]

GOLAUD

What are you doing here?

Que faites-vous ici?

PELLEAS

What am I doing here? I was . . .

Ce que je fais ici? . . . Je . . .

GOLAUD

What children you are . . . Mélisande, don't lean so far out of the window, you might fall . . . Don't you realise it's late? It's almost midnight. Don't play like that in the dark. What children you are.

Vous êtes des enfants . . . Mélisande, ne te penche pas ainsi à la fenêtre, tu vas tomber . . . Vous ne savez pas qu'il est tard? – Il est près de minuit. – Ne jouez pas ainsi dans l'obscurité. – Vous êtes des enfants . . .

(*laughing nervously*)

What children! What children!

Quels enfants! . . . Quels enfants! . . .

(*He goes out with Pelléas.*)

¹**Scene Three.** *The castle vaults. Enter Golaud and Pelléas.* [24]

GOLAUD

Be careful: follow me, follow me. Have you never been down here into these vaults?

Prenez garde: par ici, par ici. – Vous n'avez jamais pénétré dans ces souterrains?

PELLEAS

Yes, yes, I have, once before; but that was long ago . . .

Si, une fois, dans le temps; mais il y a longtemps . . .

GOLAUD

[They are prodigiously large. There's a series of enormous caves leading heaven knows where. The whole castle is built over these caves. Can you smell the deadly odour all around? That's what I wanted you to notice. My belief is that it comes from the little subterranean lake which I'll show you. Take care; walk in front of me, in the light from my lantern. I'll tell you when we get there.

[Ils sont prodigieusement grands; c'est une suite de grottes énormes qui about-issent, Dieu sait où. Tout le château est bâti sur ces grottes. Sentez-vous l'odeur mortelle qui règne ici? – C'est ce que je voulais vous faire remarquer. Selon moi, elle provient du petit lac souterrain que je vais vous faire voir. Prenez garde; marchez devant moi, dans la clarté de ma lanterne. Je vous avertirai lorsque nous y serons.

(*They continue walking in silence.*)

---

¹ Scene Two of the opera.

Hey! Hey! Pelléas! Stop, stop!   Hé! Hé! Pelléas! arrêtez! arrêtez! –

(He seizes his arm.)

Good God! Didn't you see? One more step and you'd have fallen over the edge!   Pour Dieu! . . . Mais ne voyez-vous pas? – Un pas de plus et vous étiez dans le gouffre! . . .

PELLEAS

But I didn't see it! The lantern wasn't giving any light . . .   Mais je n'y voyais pas! . . . La lanterne ne m'éclairait plus . . .

GOLAUD

I missed my footing . . . but if I hadn't held your arm . . .] Over there, there's the stagnant water I told you about . . . Can you smell the stench of death? We'll go to the edge of this rock that juts out, then you lean over; it will strike you immediately.   J'ai fait un faux pas . . . mais si je ne vous avais pas retenu par le bras . . .] Eh bien, voici l'eau stagnante dont je vous parlais . . . Sentez-vous l'odeur de mort qui monte? – Allons jusqu'au bout de ce rocher qui surplombe et penchez-vous un peu. Elle viendra vous frapper au visage.

PELLEAS

[I can smell it already . . . It's like the stench of the grave.   [Je la sens déjà . . . on dirait une odeur de tombeau.

GOLAUD

Go on a bit further . . . That's what poisons the castle from time to time. The king won't believe it comes from here. The cave where this deathly water is should be walled up. It's time to inspect these vaults, too. Do you see the cracks in the walls and in the supporting columns? Here is some hidden unsuspected work, and the whole castle will be engulfed one night if care is not taken. But what can be done? No one likes to come down this far . . . There are strange cracks in many of the walls . . . Oh! There! Can you smell the stench of death coming up?   Plus loin, plus loin . . . C'est elle qui, certains jours, empoisonne le château. Le roi ne veut pas croire qu'elle vient d'ici. – Il faudrait faire murer la grotte où se trouve cette eau morte. Il serait temps d'ailleurs d'examiner ces souterrains. Avez-vous remarqué ces lézardes dans les murs et les piliers des voûtes? – Il y a ici un travail caché qu'on ne soupçonne pas; et tout le château s'engloutira une de ces nuits, si l'on n'y prend pas garde. Mais que voulez-vous? personne n'aime à descendre jusqu'ici . . . Il y a d'étranges lézardes dans bien des murs . . . Oh! voici . . . sentez-vous l'odeur de mort qui s'élève?

PELLEAS

Yes, there's a stench of death coming up round us . . .]   Oui, il y a une odeur de mort qui monte autour de nous . . .]

GOLAUD

Lean over, don't be afraid . . . I shall hold you . . . let me hold you . . . No, no, not your hand, it might slip. Your arm. Can you see the abyss?   Penchez-vous; n'ayez pas peur . . . je vous tiendrai . . . donnez-moi . . . non, non, pas la main . . . elle pourrait glisser . . . le bras, le bras . . . Voyez-vous le gouffre?

(disturbed)

Pelléas? Pelléas?   Pelléas? Pelléas . . .

PELLEAS

Yes, I think I can see the very bottom of it! Is it the light flickering like that? Were you . . . ?   Oui; je crois que je vois le fond du gouffre . . . Est-ce la lumière qui tremble ainsi? . . . Vous . . .

(He starts, turns, and looks at Golaud.)

GOLAUD

(his voice trembling)

Yes, it's the lantern . . . You see, I was waving it to throw light on the walls . . .   Oui; c'est la lanterne . . . Voyez, je l'agitais pour éclairer les parois . . .

PELLEAS

It's stifling here . . . Let's go out.   J'étouffe ici . . . sortons . . .

Yes, let's go out.   Oui; sortons . . .

(They go out in silence.)

[1]**Scene Four.** *A terrace at the entrance of the vaults. Enter Golaud and Pelléas.*

PELLEAS

Ah! At last I can breathe! I thought for a   Ah! Je respire enfin! . . . J'ai cru, un
moment I was going to feel ill in those   instant, que j'allais me trouver mal dans
cavernous spaces; I felt on the verge of   ces énormes grottes; et je fus sur le point de
collapse . . . The very air there is heavy   tomber . . . Il y a là un air humide et lourd
and dank, like dewdrops of lead, and the   comme une rosée de plomb, et des ténèbres
darkness is dense, like a poisonous brew.   épaisses comme une pâte empoisonnée . . .
And now up here, everywhere air, fresh   Et maintenant, tout l'air de toute la mer!
from the sea! . . . How fresh the breeze!   . . . Il y a un vent frais, voyez, frais comme
Feel, feel the breeze as fresh as a newly   une feuille qui vient de s'ouvrir, sur les
opened leaf, with its tiny streaks of green.   petites lames vertes . . . Tiens! on vient
Ah! the flowers at the edge of the terrace   d'arroser les fleurs au [2]pied de la terrasse,
have been watered, and the scent of the   et l'odeur de la verdure et des roses mouillées
fresh leaves and of new-watered roses   monte jusqu'ici . . . Il doit être près de
wafts up to us here. It must be near to   midi, elles sont déjà dans l'ombre de la
noon; they're already in the shadow of   tour . . . Il est midi; j'entends sonner les
the tower. Yes, it is noon, I can hear the   cloches et les enfants descendent sur la
bells striking, and the children are going   plage pour se baigner . . . [Je ne savais pas
down to the beach to bathe . . . [I didn't   que nous fussions restés si longtemps dans
know we stayed so long down in the   les caves . . .
caves . . .

GOLAUD

We went down about eleven o'clock . . .   Nous y sommes descendus vers onze
                                                 heures . . .

PELLEAS

Earlier than that; it must have been earlier.   Plus tôt; il devait être plus tôt; j'ai entendu
I heard it strike half past ten.   sonner la demie de dix heures.

GOLAUD

Half past ten or quarter to eleven . . .   Dix heures et demie ou onze heures moins
                                                 le quart . . .

PELLEAS

All the castle windows are open. It will be   On a ouvert toutes les fenêtres du château.
especially hot this afternoon.] Look! there's   Il fera extraordinairement chaud cet après-
our mother with Mélisande at the window   midi . . .] Tiens, voilà notre mère et
in the tower . . .   Mélisande à une fenêtre de la tour . . .

GOLAUD

Yes; they have taken refuge in the shadows.   Oui; elles se sont réfugiées du côté de
Speaking of Mélisande, I overheard what   l'ombre. – A propos de Mélisande, j'ai
passed between you and what was said last   entendu ce qui s'est passé et ce qui s'est dit
night. I know quite well those are childish   hier au soir. Je le sais bien, ce sont là jeux
games; but that kind of scene must not   d'enfants; mais il ne faut pas que cela se
happen again. She is very frail, [very   répète. [Mélisande est très jeune et très
young and very impressionable] and she   impressionable],[3] et il faut qu'on la ménage
needs all the more attention now, especially   d'autant plus qu'elle [est peut-être enceinte
since she will soon be a mother; [she is very   en ce moment . . . Elle est très délicate, à
frail, scarcely grown up;] and the slightest   peine femme][4]; et la moindre émotion
emotion could have an unfortunate effect.   pourrait amener un malheur. Ce n'est pas
This is not the first time I have noticed that   la première fois que je remarque qu'il

---

[1] Scene Three of the opera.
[2] bord
[3] Elle est très délicate,
[4] sera peut-être bientôt mère,

67

there might be something between her and you. You are older than she is, I hope what I have said will suffice . . . Avoid her as much as possible, but not too obviously, of course, not too obviously. [What's that on the road there towards the forest?

pourrait y avoir quelque chose entre vous . . . vous êtes plus âgé qu'elle; il suffira de vous l'avoir dit . . . Évitez-la autant que possible, mais sans affectation d'ailleurs; sans affectation . . . [– Qu'est-ce que je vois là sur la route du côté de la forêt? . . .

PELLEAS

Those are flocks being driven to town . . .

Ce sont des troupeaux qu'on mène vers la ville . . .

GOLAUD

They're crying like lost children; they seem to scent the slaughterhouse. What a lovely day! What a fine day for the harvest!]

Ils pleurent comme des enfants perdus; on dirait qu'ils sentent déjà le boucher. – Quelle belle journée! Quelle admirable journée pour la moisson! . . .

(*They go out.*)

[1]**Scene Five.** *Before the castle. Enter Golaud and little Yniold.*

GOLAUD

Come, let's sit down here together, Yniold; come and sit on my knee. From here we can see everything that's happening in the forest. I have seen very little of you for some time. You have deserted me too. You seem to spend all your time with Mama . . . In fact this very place where we're sitting is exactly beneath her window. She is probably at her evening prayers at this moment. But tell me, Yniold, she spends a lot of time with your uncle Pelléas, doesn't she?

Viens, nous allons nous asseoir ici, Yniold; viens sur mes genoux: nous verrons d'ici ce qui se passe dans la forêt. Je ne te vois plus du tout depuis quelque temps. Tu m'abandonnes aussi; tu es toujours chez petite-mère . . . Tiens, nous sommes tout juste assis sous les fenêtres de petite-mère. – Elle fait peut-être sa prière du soir en ce moment . . . Mais dis-moi, Yniold, elle est souvent avec ton oncle Pelléas, n'est-ce pas?

YNIOLD

Yes, yes, a lot, yes, Papa; whenever you're away.

[25, 26] Oui, oui; toujours, petit-père; quand vous n'êtes pas là, petit-père . . .

GOLAUD

Look, I can see someone coming down the garden with a lantern. But I'm told they do not like each other . . . I understand that they often have quarrels . . . no? Is that true?

Ah! – Tiens; quelqu'un passe avec une lanterne dans le jardin. – Mais on m'a dit qu'ils ne s'aimaient pas . . . Il paraît qu'ils se querellent souvent . . . non? Est-ce vrai?

YNIOLD

Yes, yes, it's true.

Oui, c'est vrai.

GOLAUD

Yes? Ah, ha! In that case what are their quarrels about?

Oui? – Ah! ah! – Mais à propos de quoi se querellent-ils?

YNIOLD

About the door.

A propos de la porte.

GOLAUD

The door? They quarrel about the door, you say? [What's that you tell me? Tell me, what do you mean?] Why do they quarrel about that?

Comment? à propos de la porte? – Qu'est-ce que tu racontes là? – [Mais voyons, explique-toi; pourquoi se querellent-ils à propos de la porte?]

YNIOLD

Because they don't want it open.

Parce qu'on ne veut pas qu'elle soit ouverte.

---

[1] Scene Four of the opera.

GOLAUD

Which of them doesn't want it open? Can you tell me, why do they quarrel?	Qui ne veut pas qu'elle soit ouverte? – Voyons, pourquoi se querellent-ils?

YNIOLD

I don't know, Papa, about the light.	Je ne sais pas, petit-père, à propos de la lumière.

GOLAUD

I wasn't talking about the light: [we'll talk about that presently.] I was talking about the door. [Answer my question. You must learn to talk! It's time . . .] Don't keep putting your hand in your mouth like that . . . Come on!	Je ne te parle pas de la lumière: [nous en parlerons tout à l'heure.] Je te parle de la porte. [Réponds à ce que je te demande; tu dois apprendre à parler; il est temps . . .] Ne mets pas ainsi la main dans la bouche . . . voyons . . .

YNIOLD

Sorry, Papa! Sorry, Papa . . . I won't do it again . . .	Petit-père! petit-père! . . . Je ne le ferai plus . . .

(He starts to cry.)

GOLAUD

Now tell me: why are you beginning to cry? What makes you do that?	Voyons; pourquoi pleures-tu? Qu'est-il arrivé?

YNIOLD

Oh! Oh! Oh, Papa, you've hurt me so!	Oh! oh! petit-père, vous m'avez fait mal . . .

GOLAUD

I've hurt you so? Where have I hurt you? I didn't mean to . . .	Je t'ai fait mal? – Où t'ai-je fait mal? C'est sans le vouloir . . .

YNIOLD

Here, here on my arm . . .	Ici, à mon petit bras . . .

GOLAUD

I did not mean to. Come now, stop crying. If you do, I'll give you a present tomorrow . . .	C'est sans le vouloir; voyons, ne pleure plus, je te donnerai quelque chose demain . . .

YNIOLD

What, what, Papa?	Quoi, petit-père?

GOLAUD

Some arrows and a quiver. But tell me what you know about the door.	Un carquois et des flèches; mais dis-moi ce que tu sais [au sujet] de la porte.

YNIOLD

Will they be big arrows?	De grandes flèches?

GOLAUD

Yes, yes, they'll be very big. But why, you must tell me, why don't they want the door open? Come on, you must answer my question. No, no, open your mouth to answer, not to cry. I'm not angry with you. [We'll talk quietly, like Pelléas and Mama when they're together.] What do they talk about when they're together?	Oui, oui; de très grandes flèches. – Mais pourquoi ne veulent-ils pas que la porte soit ouverte? – Voyons, réponds-moi à la fin! – non, non; n'ouvre pas la bouche pour pleurer. Je ne suis pas fâché. [Nous allons causer tranquillement comme Pelléas et petite-mère quand ils sont ensemble.] De quoi parlent-ils quand ils sont ensemble?

YNIOLD

You mean Pelléas and Mama?	Pelléas et petite-mère?

GOLAUD

Yes; what do they talk about?	Oui; de quoi parlent-ils?

YNIOLD

Me; it's always me.	De moi; toujours de moi.

And what do they say about you?	Et que disent-ils de toi?

YNIOLD

They say that I will be very big.	Ils disent que je serai très grand.

GOLAUD

Ah! Despair and damnation! I feel like a blind man looking for his gold at the bottom of the sea! I feel like a new-born babe lost in the forest ... and you ... But come, Yniold, my mind was wandering; I must ask you some serious questions. Pelléas and Mama, do they never talk about me when I'm not there?

Ah! misère de ma vie! ... je suis ici comme un aveugle qui cherche son trésor au fond de l'océan! ... Je suis ici comme un nouveau-né perdu dans la forêt et vous ... Mais voyons, Yniold, j'étais distrait; nous allons causer sérieusement. Pelléas et petite-mère ne parlent-ils jamais de moi quand je ne suis pas là? ...

YNIOLD

Yes, yes, Papa. [They are always talking about you.]

Si, si, petit-père; [ils parlent toujours de vous.]

GOLAUD

Ah, and what do they say?	Ah! ... Et que disent-ils de moi?

YNIOLD

They say that I will grow up to be as big as you.

Ils disent que je deviendrai aussi grand que vous.

GOLAUD

Are you always very near them?	Tu es toujours près d'eux?

YNIOLD

Yes, yes, very near, yes, Papa.	Oui; oui; toujours, toujours, petit-père.

GOLAUD

Do they never tell you, run away and play?	Ils ne te disent jamais d'aller jouer ailleurs?

YNIOLD

No, no, Papa; they're afraid when I'm not there.

Non, petit-père; ils ont peur quand je ne suis pas là.

GOLAUD

They're afraid? How can you tell they're afraid?

Ils ont peur? ... à quoi vois-tu qu'ils ont peur?

YNIOLD

[Mama says all the time, 'Don't go, don't go!' ... They're unhappy, but they smile.

[Petite-mère qui dit toujours: ne t'en va pas, ne t'en va pas ... Ils sont malheureux, mais ils rient ...

GOLAUD

But that doesn't mean they're frightened.	Mais cela ne prouve pas qu'ils aient peur.

YNIOLD

Yes, yes, Papa. She's frightened ...	Si, si, petit-père; elle a peur ...

GOLAUD

Why do you say she's frightened?]	Pourquoi dis-tu qu'elle a peur?]

YNIOLD

They cry all the time in the darkness.	Ils pleurent toujours dans l'obscurité.

GOLAUD

Ah, ha!	Ah! ah! ...

YNIOLD

And that makes me cry too ...	Cela fait pleurer aussi ...

GOLAUD

Yes, yes!	Oui, oui ...

Yes, Papa, she's so pale, Papa!

Elle est pâle, petit-père.

Ah! Ah, give me patience, my God, give me[27] patience . . .

Ah! ah! . . . patience, mon Dieu, patience . . .

What, Papa?

Quoi, petit-père?

Nothing, nothing, it was nothing. A wolf just went by in the forest. [So they're happy together? I'm pleased to learn that they are friendly.] Do they sometimes kiss? No?

Rien, rien, mon enfant. – J'ai vu passer un loup dans la forêt. – [Alors ils s'entendent bien? – Je suis heureux d'apprendre qu'ils sont d'accord. –] Ils s'embrassent quelque-fois? – Non?

Do they kiss sometimes? No, Papa, no, no. Oh! yes, Papa, yes, once, once, when it was raining . . .

Qu'ils s'embrassent, petit-père? – Non, non. –Ah! si, petit-père, si, si; une fois . . . une fois qu'il pleuvait . . .

You say that they kissed? Are you sure? But how? In what way did they kiss?

Ils se sont embrassés? – Mais comment, comment se sont-ils embrassés? –

Just like this, see, Papa, just like this.

Comme ça, petit-père, comme ça! . . .

(*He kisses him on the mouth, laughing.*)

Oh! Oh! Your beard, Papa! It's your beard, Papa! It tickles! It tickles! Look how grey your beard's growing. Look, look, Papa! And so too is your hair! All grey, all grey!

Ah! ah! votre barbe, petit-père! . . . Elle pique! elle pique! Elle devient toute grise, petit-père, et vos cheveux aussi; tout gris, tout gris . . .

(*At that moment a light appears in the window above where they are sitting and its light falls on them.*) [28]

Oh look! Mama has lighted the lamp in her window. Now it's light. Look, Papa, now it's light.

Ah! ah! petite-mère a allumé sa lampe. Il fait clair, petit-père; il fait clair.

Yes, it's beginning to get light.

Oui; il commence à faire clair . . .

Let's go in there too. In there, Papa; let's go in there too.

Allons-y aussi, petit-père . . .

Where do you want to go?

Où veux-tu aller?

Where the light is, up there, Papa.

Où il fait clair, petit-père.

No, no, my child; we'll stay out here a while in the darkness . . . You never know, you never know for certain . . . [Can you see those beggars trying to light a fire in the forest? It's been raining. On the other side, can you see the old gardener trying to shift the tree blown across the road by the wind? He can't; the tree's too big, the tree's too heavy, and it will stay where it fell. Nothing can be done about it.] I do believe Pelléas is mad.

Non, non, mon enfant: restons encore un peu dans l'ombre . . . on ne sait pas . . . on ne sait pas encore . . . [Vois-tu là-bas ces pauvres qui essaient d'allumer un petit feu dans la forêt? – Il a plu. Et de l'autre côté, vois-tu le vieux jardinier qui essaie de soulever cet arbre que le vent a jeté en travers du chemin? – Il ne peut pas; l'arbre est trop grand; l'arbre est trop lourd, et il restera du côté où il est tombé. Il n'y a rien à faire à tout cela . . .] Je crois que Pelléas est fou . . .

No, no, no, Papa, he isn't mad, but he's very kind.

Non, petit-père, il n'est pas fou, mais il est très bon.

GOLAUD

Would you like to see Mama?

Veux-tu voir petite-mère?

YNIOLD

Yes, yes, I would love to!

Oui, oui; je veux la voir!

GOLAUD

Don't make a sound. I'll lift you up as far as the window. It is too high for me, even though I'm so tall ...

Ne fais pas de bruit; je vais te hisser jusqu'à la fenêtre. Elle est trop haute pour moi, bien que je sois si grand ...

(*He lifts the child up.*)

Don't make the slightest sound; Mama would have a terrible fright if she heard you. Do you see her? Is she in the room?

Ne fais pas le moindre bruit; petite-mère aurait terriblement peur ... La vois-tu? – Est-elle dans la chambre?

YNIOLD

Yes ... Oh! It's so bright!

Oui ... Oh! il fait clair!

GOLAUD

Is she alone in there?

Elle est seule?

YNIOLD

Yes ... No, no! My uncle Pelléas is in there too.

Oui ... non, non; mon oncle Pelléas y est aussi.

GOLAUD

He ...

Il! ...

YNIOLD

Oh, oh, oh, Papa, you're hurting me!

Ah! ah! petit-père! vous m'avez fait mal! ...

GOLAUD

Never mind, be quiet, I won't do that again; look, look, Yniold! I nearly slipped. Speak very quietly. What are they doing?

Ce n'est rien; tais-toi; je ne le ferai plus; regarde, regarde, Yniold! ... J'ai trébuché; parle plus bas. Que font-ils? –

YNIOLD

They're not doing anything, Papa. [They're waiting for something.]

Ils ne font rien, petit-père; [ils attendent quelque chose.]

GOLAUD

Are they close to each other?

Sont-ils près l'un de l'autre?

YNIOLD

No, no, Papa.

Non, petit-père.

GOLAUD

And ... And the bed? Are they near the bed?

Et ... Et le lit? sont-ils près du lit?

YNIOLD

The bed, Papa? I cannot see the bed.

Le lit, petit-père? – Je ne vois pas le lit.

GOLAUD

Not so loud; they'll hear you. Are they speaking?

Plus bas, plus bas; ils t'entendraient. Est-ce qu'ils parlent?

YNIOLD

No, no, Papa, they're not speaking.

Non, petit-père; ils ne parlent pas.

GOLAUD

But what are they doing? [They must be doing something.]

Mais que font-ils? [– Il faut qu'ils fassent quelque chose ...]

YNIOLD

They are looking at the light.

Ils regardent la lumière.

Both of them?   Tous les deux?

YNIOLD

Yes, yes, Papa.   Oui, petit-père.

GOLAUD

Aren't they saying anything?   Ils ne disent rien?

YNIOLD

No, no, Papa; they don't shut their eyes.   Non, petit-père; ils ne ferment pas les yeux.

GOLAUD

Aren't they getting close to each other?   Ils ne s'approchent pas l'un de l'autre?

YNIOLD

No, no, Papa; [they're not moving.   Non, petit-père, [ils ne bougent pas.

GOLAUD

Are they sitting down?   Ils sont assis?

YNIOLD

No, Papa, they're standing by the wall.   Non, petit-père; ils sont debout contre le mur.

GOLAUD

Are they making gestures? Are they looking at each other? Are they making signs?   Ils ne font pas de gestes? – Ils ne se regardent pas? – Ils ne font pas de signes?

YNIOLD

No, Papa; oh, oh! Papa,] they don't shut their eyes at all. I'm terribly afraid!   Non, petit-père. – Oh! oh! petit-père,] ils ne ferment jamais les yeux . . . J'ai terriblement peur . . .

GOLAUD

[Quiet! Are they still not moving?   [Tais-toi. Ils ne bougent pas encore?

YNIOLD

No, Papa. I'm frightened, Papa, let me down!]   Non, petit-père – j'ai peur, petit-père, laissez-moi descendre!]

GOLAUD

What are you afraid of? Keep looking. Keep looking!   De quoi donc as-tu peur? – Regarde! regarde! . . .

YNIOLD

[I daren't keep looking!] No, Papa, please let me get down now!   [Je n'ose plus regarder,] petit-père! . . . Laissez-moi descendre! . . .

GOLAUD

Keep looking!   Regarde! [regarde!]

YNIOLD

Oh, I want to scream, to scream, Papa! Please let me get down now! Please let me get down now!   Oh! oh! je vais crier, petit-père! – Laissez-moi descendre! laissez-moi descendre! . . .

GOLAUD

Come on! [We'll go and see what's happened.]   Viens [nous allons voir ce qui est arrivé].

(*They go out.*)

Act Four

Scene One.[1] *A passage in the castle. Pelléas and Mélisande enter and meet.* [29]

PELLEAS

Where are you going? I must speak to you this evening. Will I see you?

Où vas-tu? Il faut que je te parle ce soir. Te verrai-je?

MELISANDE

Yes.

Oui.

PELLEAS

I have come from my father's bedside. He is better. The doctor has told us he is saved ... [But this morning I had a foreboding that today would end badly. For some time I've been hearing disaster in my ears ... Then there was suddenly a change; today it's just a matter of time. All the windows of his room are open. He can speak; he seems content. He does not speak yet like a normal man, but his thoughts no longer seem to come all from the other world ...] He knew who I was. He took my hand and said in that strange manner which he has had since his illness: "Is it you, Pelléas? Listen, I have never noticed it before, but you have that grave and friendly appearance of one who will not live for very long. You must see the world, you must see the world ...". It's strange, I shall obey him. My mother heard him speak and wept with joy. Have you not noticed the difference? The whole house seems to have come to life again. One can hear breathing, [one can hear voices,] one can even hear movement ... Listen closely, I can hear someone's voice behind that door. Quick then, quick, tell me quickly, where shall I see you?

Je sors de la chambre de mon père. Il va mieux. Le médecin nous a dit qu'il était sauvé ... [Ce matin cependant j'avais le pressentiment que cette journée finirait mal. J'ai depuis quelque temps un bruit de malheur dans les oreilles ... Puis, il y eut tout à coup un grand revirement; aujourd'hui ce n'est plus qu'une question de temps. On a ouvert toutes les fenêtres de sa chambre. Il parle; il semble heureux. Il ne parle pas encore comme un homme ordinaire, mais déjà ses idées ne viennent plus toutes de l'autre monde ...] Il m'a reconnu. Il m'a pris la main, et il m'a dit de cet air étrange qu'il a depuis qu'il est malade: "Est-ce toi, Pelléas? Tiens, tiens, je ne l'avais jamais remarqué, mais tu as le visage grave et amical de ceux qui ne vivront pas longtemps ... Il faut voyager; il faut voyager ..." C'est étrange; je vais lui obéir ... Ma mère l'écoutait et pleurait de joie. – Tu ne t'en es pas aperçue? – Toute la maison semble déjà revivre, on entend respirer, [on entend parler,] on entend marcher ... Ecoute, j'entends parler derrière cette porte. Vite, vite, réponds vite, où te verrai-je?

MELISANDE

Where would you like?

Ou veux-tu?

PELLEAS

In the park by the well, by the Blind Man's Well? You will? Will you come?

Dans le parc; près de la fontaine des aveugles? – Veux-tu? – viendras-tu?

MELISANDE

Yes.

Oui.

PELLEAS

This evening will be our last. I am going on my travels as my father told me. You will not see me again ...

Ce sera le dernier soir; – je vais voyager comme mon père l'a dit. Tu ne me verras plus ...

MELISANDE

Don't say that, Pelléas ... I will see you for ever; I will look at you for ever ...

Ne dis pas cela, Pelléas ... Je te verrai toujours; je te regarderai toujours ...

---

[1] *A room*

74

There will be no purpose in looking ... I'll be so far away that you won't be able to see me ... [I'll try to go far away ... I am full of joy and I feel I have the whole weight of heaven and earth on my body.]

Tu auras beau regarder ... je serai si loin que tu ne pourras plus me voir ... [Je vais tâcher d'aller très loin ... Je suis plein de joie et l'on dirait que j'ai tout le poids du ciel et de la terre sur le corps.]

MELISANDE

What has happened, Pelléas? I no longer understand what you say.

Qu'est-il arrivé, Pelléas? – Je ne comprends plus ce que tu dis ...

PELLEAS

Now go. We must not stay. I hear someone's voice behind that door. [It is the visitors who came to the castle this morning ... They're leaving ... Let's go; it's the visitors ...]

Va-t'en, va t'en, séparons-nous. J'entends parler derrière cette porte ... [Ce sont les étrangers qui sont arrivés au château ce matin ... Ils vont sortir ... Allons-nous-en; ce sont les étrangers ...]

[(*They go out separately.*)]

Scene Two. [*A room in the castle.*] [1]*Arkel and Mélisande are discovered.*

ARKEL

Now that Pelléas's father has recovered, and now that the sickness, that faithful servant of death, has departed from the castle, glimmers of happiness, glimmers of sunlight may at last come back into our house ... Not before time! For ever since you came, we have done nothing here but move in whispers round the sick man's chamber ... On my word I was sorry for [30] you, Mélisande ... [You came here full of joy like a child going to a party. The moment you came into the entrance hall I saw your face change, probably your soul too, the way one's face changes of its own accord when one goes into a cold, dark cave in the middle of the day ... Since then, because of that, I have often not understood you ...] I have been watching you since you came, you were heedless perhaps, yet with that strange distracted air of one who expects misfortune at any moment, even in the garden in the sunshine ... I cannot explain ... But it has disturbed me to see you thus, for you are too young and too beautiful to spend all your days and your nights in an atmosphere of death ... But from now on all these things will change. In my old age – and this perhaps is the surest blessing of a lifetime – in my old age I have learnt in a curious way to rely on the certainty of destiny, for I have observed how anyone young and beautiful always draws to himself a destiny young, beautiful and happy ... Now it is you who will open the door upon the new era which I foresee. Come here; why do you not answer me, then, nor even raise your eyes? Only once have I kissed you before, and that was the very day you first arrived; yet nonetheless

Maintenant que le père de Pelléas est sauvé, et que la maladie, la vieille servante de la mort, a quitté le château, un peu de joie et un peu de soleil vont enfin rentrer dans la maison ... Il était temps! – Car depuis ta venue, on n'a vécu ici qu'en chuchotant autour d'une chambre fermée... Et vraiment, j'avais pitié de toi, Mélisande ... [Tu arrivais ici, toute joyeuse, comme un enfant à la recherche d'une fête, et au moment où tu entrais dans la vestibule, je t'ai vue changer de visage, et probablement d'âme, comme on change de visage, malgré soi, lorsqu'on entre à midi, dans une grotte trop sombre et trop froide ... Et depuis, à cause de tout cela, souvent, je ne te comprenais plus ...] Je t'observais, tu étais là, insouciante peut-être, mais avec l'air étrange et égaré de quelqu'un qui attendrait toujours un grand malheur, au soleil, dans un beau jardin ... Je ne puis pas expliquer ... Mais j'étais triste de te voir ainsi; car tu es trop jeune et trop belle pour vivre déjà, jour et nuit, sous l'haleine de la mort ... Mais à présent tout cela va changer. A mon âge, – et c'est peut-être le fruit le plus sûr de ma vie, – à mon âge, j'ai acquis je ne sais quelle foi à la fidélité des événements, et j'ai toujours vu que tout être jeune et beau, créait autour de lui des événements jeunes, beaux et heureux ... Et c'est toi, maintenant, qui va ouvrir la porte à l'ère nouvelle que j'entrevois ... Viens ici; pourquoi restes-tu là sans repondre et sans lever les yeux? – Je ne t'ai embrassée qu'une seule fois jusqu'ici, le jour de ta venue; et cependant, les

---

[1] (*Enter Arkel.*)

an old man such as I needs now and again to touch a woman's brow or a child's cheek with his lips, to reassure himself that life has not lost its freshness, and for a moment to delay the threat of death. Tell me, do my old lips alarm you? Lately I have felt such pity for you . . .

vieillards ont besoin de toucher quelque-fois de leurs lèvres, le front d'une femme ou la joue d'un enfant, pour croire encore à la fraîcheur de la vie et éloigner un moment les menaces de la mort. As-tu peur de mes vieilles lèvres? Comme j'avais pitié de toi ces mois-ci! . . .

MELISANDE

Grandfather, I have not been unhappy.

Grand-père, je n'étais pas malheureuse . . .

ARKEL

[Perhaps you are one of those people who can be unhappy without knowing it . . .] Let me look at you again like this, come closer for a moment . . . One has such a need for beauty when near to death . . .

[Peut-être étais-tu de celles qui sont malheureuses sans le savoir . . .] Laisse-moi te regarder ainsi, de tout près, un moment . . . on a un tel besoin de beauté aux côtés de la mort . . .

(Enter Golaud.)

GOLAUD

Pelléas leaves tonight.

Pelléas part ce soir.

ARKEL

You have blood on your forehead. What have you done?

Tu as du sang sur le front. – Qu'as-tu fait?

GOLAUD

Nothing, nothing . . . I scratched myself when I went through a thornbush.

Rien, rien . . . j'ai passé au travers d'une haie d'épines.

MELISANDE

Will you lower your head, my lord . . . I will wipe your brow . . .

Baissez un peu la tête, seigneur . . . Je vais essuyer votre front . . .

GOLAUD
(pushing her back)

I don't want you to touch me, do you hear? Get off! I am not addressing you. Where's my sword? I came here to fetch my sword . . .

Je ne veux pas que tu me touches, entends-tu? Va-t'en, va-t'en! – Je ne te parle pas. – Où est mon épée? – Je venais chercher mon épée . . .

MELISANDE

It is here, on the prie-Dieu.

Ici; sur le prie-Dieu.

GOLAUD

Bring it here.
(to Arkel)

Apporte-la. –

Another peasant has just been found down by the sea, dead of starvation. One would think they all mean to die before our very eyes.

On vient encore de trouver un paysan mort de faim, le long de la mer. On dirait qu'ils tiennent tous à mourir sous nos yeux. –

(to Mélisande)

Come now, my sword? Why are you trembling like that? I'm not going to kill you. I only wanted to examine the blade. I would not use a sword for such a purpose. Why do you examine me as if I were a beggar? I am not begging any charity from you. Do you think you'll see something in my eyes while things in your eyes, you hope, escape my notice? Do you think I know something?

Eh bien, mon épée? – Pourquoi tremblez-vous ainsi? – Je ne vais pas vous tuer. Je voulais simplement examiner la lame. Je n'emploie pas l'épée à ces usages. Pourquoi m'examinez-vous comme un pauvre? – Je ne viens pas vous demander l'aumône. Vous espérez voir quelque chose dans mes yeux, sans que je voie quelque chose dans les vôtres? – Croyez-vous que je sache quelque chose? –

(to Arkel)

Look at those great eyes. One would say they were proud of their beauty.

Voyez-vous ces grands yeux? – On dirait qu'ils sonts fiers d'être riches . . .

I see nothing in them but innocence . . .

Je n'y vois qu'une grande innocence . . .

GOLAUD

Nothing in them but innocence! . . . They are bigger than innocence. They are purer than the eyes of a lamb . . . They could give the Almighty a lesson in innocence! Nothing in them but innocence! See here: I am so close to her that I can feel the fluttering of her eyelids; yet nonetheless I am nearer to the secrets of the other world than to the smallest secret of those eyes: nothing in them but innocence! More in them than innocence! There one might see celebration of baptism attended by heavenly angels. I know them well, those eyes! I have seen them at work! Shut them! Shut them! If you don't, then I'll shut them myself . . . Don't keep putting your [right] hand to your throat like that. I'll tell you something very simple . . . I have no ulterior motive . . . If I had an ulterior motive why would I not say at once? Ah, ah! Don't try to escape! Come here! Give me your hand! Ah! Your hands are too hot . . . Out of my way! Your flesh disgusts me! Out of my way! It's no longer a question of escape!

Une grande innocence! . . . Ils sont plus grands que l'innocence! . . . Ils sont plus purs que les yeux d'un agneau . . . Ils donneraient à Dieu des leçons d'innocence! Une grande innocence! Ecoutez: j'en suis si près que je sens la fraîcheur de leurs cils quand ils clignent; et cependant, je suis moins loin des grands secrets de l'autre monde que du plus petit secret de ces yeux! . . . Une grande innocence! . . . Plus que de l'innocence! On dirait que les anges du ciel y célèbrent sans cesse un baptême! . . . Je les connais ces yeux! Je les ai vus à l'oeuvre! Fermez-les! fermez-les! ou je vais les fermer pour longtemps! . . . – Ne mettez pas ainsi la main [droite] à la gorge; je dis une chose très simple . . . Je n'ai pas d'arrière-pensée . . . Si j'avais une arrière-pensée, pourquoi ne la dirais-je pas? Ah! ah! – ne tâchez pas de fuir! – Ici! – Donnez-moi cette main! –Ah! vos mains sont trop chaudes . . . Allez-vous-en! Votre chair me dégoûte! . . . [1]Ici! –Il ne s'agit plus de fuir à présent!

(He seizes her by the hair.)

You can follow me on your knees! Get down on your knees! Ah, ha! So your long hair may after all be good for something. Right then left! Left then right! Absalom! Absalom! Forward and back! On the ground there! On the ground there! . . . Now you see! Now you see! I already laugh like an old man . . . Ha, ha, ha!

Vous allez me suivre à genoux! – A genoux! – A genoux devant moi! – Ah! ah! vos longs cheveux servent enfin à quelque chose! . . . À droite et puis à gauche! – À gauche et puis à droite! – Absalon! Absalon! – En avant! en arrière! Jusqu'à terre! jusqu'à terre! . . . Vous voyez, vous voyez; je ris déjà comme un vieillard . . .

ARKEL
(stepping forward)

Golaud!

Golaud!

GOLAUD
(suddenly becoming calm)

You will do whatever you choose, to be sure. This seems to me of no particular moment. I am too old; what's more, I am not a spy. I shall leave it to chance. And then . . . Oh! Well then! . . . I mean simply because it's the custom, simply because it's the custom . . .

Vous ferez comme il vous plaira, voyez-vous. – Je n'attache aucune importance à cela. – Je suis trop vieux; et puis, je ne suis pas un espion. J'attendrai le hasard; et alors . . . Oh! alors! . . . simplement parce que c'est l'usage, simplement parce que c'est l'usage . . .

(He goes out.)

ARKEL

What's wrong with him? Is he drunk?

Qu'a-t-il donc? – Il est ivre?

MELISANDE
(in tears)

No, no, but he loves me no more . . . I am not happy . . .

Non, non; mais il ne m'aime plus . . . Je ne suis pas heureuse! . . . Je ne suis pas heureuse! . . .

---

[1] Allez-vous-en!

If I were God, I would have pity on the human heart ...

Si j'étais Dieu, j'aurais pitié du coeur des hommes ...

Scene Three. [1][*The castle terrace.*] *Little Yniold is discovered attempting to lift a boulder.*

YNIOLD

Oh! This stone's so heavy! It's much heavier than I am ... It's much heavier than everyone ... It's much heavier than everything ... I can see my ball there between that rock and this big stupid stone, and no matter how, I can't reach it. My little arm isn't long enough, and this stone is so big it doesn't want to move at all ... [I can't lift it ... Nobody can lift it ... It's heavier than the whole house ...] You would think it had great long roots in the ground ...

[31] Oh! cette pierre est lourde! ... Elle est plus lourde que moi ... Elle est plus lourde que tout le monde ... Elle est plus lourde que tout ... Je vois ma balle d'or entre le roc et cette méchante pierre, et ne puis pas l'atteindre ... Mon petit bras n'est pas assez long ... et cette pierre ne peut pas être soulevée ... [Je ne puis pas la soulever ... et personne ne pourra la soulever ... Elle est plus lourde que toute la maison ...] on dirait qu'elle a des racines dans la terre ...

(Sheep are heard bleating in the distance.)

Oh! Oh! I can hear sheep crying ...

Oh! oh! j'entends pleurer les moutons ...

[(*He crosses to the edge of the terrace to look.*)]

Look! The sun is going in ... I can see the little sheep coming! I can see them ... What a lot! Look what a lot! They're scared of the dark ... They're close together! Much too close! [They can hardly move! ...] They're crying! ... And they're hurrying! ... [They've already reached the big cross-roads. Ah! Ah! They don't know where they're supposed to go ... They've stopped crying ... They're waiting ...] There are some there which keep pushing sideways. It seems they all keep going sideways ... But they can't! The shepherd is throwing earth at them! Oh! Oh! Now they are coming this way ... [They're obeying! They're obeying! They'll pass by beneath the terrace ... beneath the rocks ...] I'll see them from close by ... [Oh! oh!] What a lot there are! [What a lot!] The whole road is full of them ...] Now they're not making any more noise ... Shepherd! Why don't they talk any more?

Tiens! il n'y a plus de soleil ... Ils arrivent, les petits moutons; ils arrivent ... Il y en a! ... il y en a! ... Ils ont peur du noir ... Ils se serrent! ... [Ils ne peuvent presque plus marcher ...] Ils pleurent! [ils pleurent!] et ils vont vite! ... [Ils sont déjà au grand carrefour. Ah! ah! ils ne savent plus par où ils doivent aller ... Ils ne pleurent plus ... Ils attendent ...] Il y en a qui voudraient prendre à droite ... Ils voudraient tous aller à droite ... Ils ne peuvent pas! ... Le berger leur jette de la terre! Ah! ah! ils vont passer par ici ... [Ils obéissent! Ils obéissent! Ils vont passer sous la terrasse ... Ils vont passer sous les rochers ...] Je vais les voir de près ... [Oh! oh!] comme il y en a! ... [Il y en a! ... Toute la route en est pleine ...] Maintenant ils se taissent tous ... Berger! berger! pourquoi ne parlent-ils plus?

SHEPHERD
(off-stage)

Because this is not the way to the sheep-fold ...

Parce que ce n'est pas le chemin de l'étable ...

YNIOLD

Where're they going? Shepherd? Shepherd? Where're they going? He can't hear me. They're already too far away ... [They're hurrying ...] They're not making any noise ... This is not the way to the sheep-fold ... Then where will they sleep for the night? Oh, oh! It's too dark ... I have something to tell someone ...

[32] Où vont-ils? – Berger! berger! – où vont-ils? – Il ne m'entend plus. Ils sont déjà trop loin ... [Ils vont vite ...] Ils ne font plus de bruit ... Ce n'est plus le chemin de l'étable ... Où vont-ils dormir cette nuit? – Oh! oh! – Il fait trop noir ... Je vais dire quelque chose à quelqu'un ...

(He goes out.)

---

[1] A well in the park

78

Scene Four. [*A well in the park.*] *Enter Pelléas.* [33]

PELLEAS

This is our last evening ... our last evening ... Everything must finish ... I've been playing like a child near something of whose existence I had no idea ... I've been playing in a dream around the pitfalls of destiny ... What is it that woke me so suddenly? I shall flee with a cry of joy and a cry of pain, like a blind man fleeing terrified from his burning house ... I'll tell her I'm going to flee ... [My father is out of danger; I have no more need to lie to myself ...] It is late; she's not coming ... It would be better if I left without seeing her again ... This time I must look at her more closely than ever ... There are certain things about her I already forget. At times you would think it was at least a hundred years since I last saw her ... And I have still not seen my eyes reflected in hers ... If I leave like that I'll have nothing to keep. And all these memories; that would be like using a muslin bag to carry water. I must look on her one last time to the depths of her heart ... I must tell her everything I have never told her ...

C'est le dernier soir ... le dernier soir ... Il faut que tout finisse ... J'ai joué comme un enfant autour d'une chose que je ne soupçonnais pas ... J'ai joué en rêve autour des pièges de la destinée ... Qui est-ce qui m'a réveillé tout à coup? Je vais fuir en criant de joie et de douleur comme un aveugle qui fuirait l'incendie de sa maison ... Je vais lui dire que je vais fuir ... [Mon père est hors de danger; et je n'ai plus de quoi me mentir à moi-même ...] Il est tard; elle ne vient pas ... Je ferais mieux de m'en aller sans la revoir ... Il faut que je la regarde bien cette fois-ci ... Il y a des choses que je ne me rappelle plus ... on dirait, par moments, qu'il y a plus de cent ans que je ne l'ai plus vue ... Et je n'ai pas encore regardé son regard ... Il ne me reste rien si je m'en vais ainsi. Et tous ces souvenirs ... c'est comme si j'emportais un peu d'eau dans un sac de mousseline ... Il faut que je la voie une dernière fois, jusqu'au fond de son coeur ... Il faut que je lui dise tout ce que je n'ai pas dit ...

(Enter Mélisande.)[34]

MELISANDE

Pelléas!

Pelléas!

PELLEAS

Mélisande! Is that you, Mélisande?

Mélisande! – Est-ce toi, Mélisande?

MELISANDE

Yes.

Oui.

PELLEAS

Come here. Don't stay there, it's too bright in the moonlight. Come here. We have so much to say to each other ... Come here, in the shadow of the trees.

Viens ici: ne reste pas au bord du clair de lune. – Viens ici. Nous avons tant de choses à nous dire ... Viens ici dans l'ombre du tilleul.

MELISANDE

Let me stay here in the light ...

Laissez-moi dans la clarté ...

PELLEAS

They could see us there from the windows of the tower. Come here, there's nothing here to be afraid of. Be careful, they could see us from there!

On pourrait nous voir des fenêtres de la tour. Viens ici; ici, nous n'avons rien à craindre. – Prends garde; on pourrait nous voir ...

MELISANDE

Let them see me then.

Je veux qu'on me voie ...

PELLEAS

Why do you say that? Were you able to get out without being seen?

Qu'as tu donc? – Tu as pu sortir sans qu'on s'en soit aperçu?

MELISANDE

Yes; your brother was asleep ...

Oui; votre frère dormait ...

It's late, in one hour the gates will be closed. We have to be careful. Why were you so late in coming?

Il est tard. – Dans une heure on fermera les portes. Il faut prendre garde. Pourquoi es-tu venue si tard?

MELISANDE

Because your brother had a nightmare. Then as I left, my dress got caught on the nails of the gate. You see where it's torn. I'd lost so much time ... so I ran ...

Votre frère avait un mauvais rêve. Et puis ma robe s'est accrochée aux clous de la porte. Voyez, elle est déchirée. J'ai perdu tout ce temps et j'ai couru ...

PELLEAS

My poor Mélisande! I almost feel afraid to touch you ... You are still out of breath, like a hunted bird ... Is it for me you've done this, is it for me? I can hear your heart beating, as though it were my own ... Come here ... Come close to me ...

Ma pauvre Mélisande! ... J'aurais presque peur de te toucher ... Tu es encore hors d'haleine comme un oiseau pourchassé ... C'est pour moi, pour moi que tu fais tout cela? ... J'entends battre ton coeur comme si c'était le mien ... Viens ici ... plus près, plus près de moi ...

MELISANDE

Why are you smiling?

Pourquoi riez-vous?

PELLEAS

I'm not smiling; or rather I'm smiling for joy, yet not aware ... Surely there's more to weep for than to smile for ...

Je ne ris pas; – ou bien je ris de joie, sans le savoir ... Il y aurait plutôt de quoi pleurer ...

MELISANDE

We came here a long time ago. I remember ...

Nous sommes venus ici il y a bien long-temps ... Je me rappelle ...

PELLEAS

Yes, that was long months ago. At that time I did not know ... Do you know why I have asked you to come this evening?

Oui ... oui ... Il y a de longs mois. – Alors, je ne savais pas ... Sais-tu pourquoi je t'ai demandé de venir ce soir?

MELISANDE

No.

Non.

PELLEAS

This is possibly the very last time I will see you. I must go away for ever ...

C'est peut-être la dernière fois que je te vois ... Il faut que je m'en aille pour toujours ...

MELISANDE

Why do you always say you're going away?

Pourquoi dis-tu toujours que tu t'en vas? ...

PELLEAS

Must I tell you what you already know? Do you not know what I have to tell you?

Je dois te dire ce que tu sais déjà? – Tu ne sais pas ce que je vais te dire?

MELISANDE

No, I don't; I know nothing.

Mais non, mais non; je ne sais rien ...

PELLEAS

Do you not know the reason why I have to leave you? Do you not know that it's because ...

Tu ne sais pas pourquoi il faut que je m'éloigne ... Tu ne sais pas que c'est parce que ...

(He kisses her suddenly.)

I love you ...

[35] Je t'aime ...

MELISANDE
(in a low voice)

I love you too ...

Je t'aime aussi ...

PELLEAS

Oh, what was that Mélisande? I could hardly hear what you said . . . We have broken the ice with red hot irons! Your voice when you said that came from the end of the earth! . . . I could hardly hear what you said . . . You love me? You love me too? How long have you loved me?

Oh! Qu'as-tu dit, Mélisande! . . . Je ne l'ai presque pas entendu! . . . On a brisé la glace avec des fers rougis! . . . Tu dis cela d'une voix qui vient du bout du monde! . . . Je ne t'ai presque pas entendue . . . Tu m'aimes? – Tu m'aimes aussi? . . . Depuis quand m'aimes tu?

MELISANDE

For ever . . . Ever since I first saw you . . .

Depuis toujours . . . Depuis que je t'ai vu . . .

PELLEAS

[Oh! The way you say that!] It is as if your voice had come over the sea in the spring! [36] I have never heard it until today. It's as though it had rained on my heart! You said those words so openly! . . . Like an angel answering questions . . . I can scarcely believe it, Mélisande . . . Why should you love me? Why do you love me? Is it true what you say? Were you making it up? Were you lying to me just to make me feel happy?

[Oh! comme tu dis cela! . . .] On dirait que ta voix a passé sur la mer au printemps! . . . je ne l'ai jamais entendue jusqu'ici . . . on dirait qu'il a plu sur mon cœur! Tu dis cela si franchement! . . . Comme un ange qu'on interroge! Je ne puis pas le croire, Mélisande . . . Pourquoi m'aimerais-tu? – Mais pourquoi m'aimes tu? – Est-ce vrai ce que tu dis? – Tu ne me trompes pas? – Tu ne mens pas un peu, pour me faire sourire? . . .

MELISANDE

No, I never tell lies; I only lie to your brother . . .

Non; je ne mens jamais; je ne mens qu'à ton frère . . .

PELLEAS

Oh! The way you say that! Your voice, your voice! It is as fresh and as clear as water! . . . It is like pure spring water on my lips. It is like pure spring water on my hands. Give me your hands, let me take your hands . . . Oh! Your hands are so tiny! I never knew you were so beautiful. I had never set eyes on anything as beautiful before . . . I could not rest, I kept searching everywhere in the house. I kept searching everywhere in the country, but never found the beauty I sought . . . And now at last I have found you. I have found you. I don't believe there is anywhere on earth a woman more beautiful . . . Where are you? I can't hear your breathing any more . . .

Oh! comme tu dis cela! . . . Ta voix! ta voix! . . . Elle est plus fraîche et plus franche que l'eau! . . . On dirait de l'eau pure sur mes lèvres! . . . On dirait de l'eau pure sur mes mains . . . Donne-moi, donne-moi tes mains . . . Oh! tes mains sont petites! . . . Je ne savais pas que tu étais si belle! . . . Je n'avais jamais rien vu d'aussi beau, avant toi . . . J'étais inquiet, je cherchais partout dans la maison . . . je cherchais partout dans la campagne . . . Et je ne trouvais pas la beauté . . . Et maintenant je t'ai trouvée! . . . Je t'ai trouvée! . . . Je ne crois pas qu'il y ait sur la terre une femme plus belle! . . . Où est-tu? – Je ne t'entends plus respirer . . .

MELISANDE

That's because I'm looking at you . . .

C'est que je te regarde . . .

PELLEAS

Why are you looking at me so seriously? The shadows have now deepened. It's too dark under the trees here. Come here where it's lighter. There in the dark we cannot see how happy we are. Come, come, we have so little time . . .

Pourquoi me regardes-tu si gravement? – Nous sommes déjà dans l'ombre. – Il fait trop noir sous cet arbre. Viens dans la lumière. Nous ne pouvons pas voir combien nous sommes heureux. Viens, viens; il nous reste si peu de temps . . .

MELISANDE

No, no; let's stay here . . . We are much closer in the darkness . . .

Non, non; restons ici . . . Je suis plus près de toi dans l'obscurité . . .

Where are your eyes? You're not going to run away? Your thoughts are not with me at this moment.

Où sont tes yeux? – Tu ne vas pas me fuir? – Tu ne songes pas à moi en ce moment.

MELISANDE

They are! They are all with you!

Mais si, mais si, je ne songe qu'à toi . . .

PELLEAS

Your eyes were somewhere else . . .

Tu regardais ailleurs . . .

MELISANDE

I saw you somewhere else . . .

Je te voyais ailleurs . . .

PELLEAS

You're not at ease. What's the matter? You seem unhappy.

Tu es distraite . . . Qu'as-tu donc? – Tu ne me sembles pas heureuse . . .

MELISANDE

No, no, I am happy, but I am sad . . .

Si, si; je suis heureuse, mais je suis triste . . .

PELLEAS

[People are often sad when they are in love . . .

[On est triste, souvent, quand on s'aime . . .

MELISANDE

I always weep when I think of you . . .

Je pleure toujours lorsque je songe à toi . . .

PELLEAS

So do I, so do I, Mélisande . . . I am close to you; I'm weeping with joy . . . and yet . . .

Moi aussi . . . moi aussi, Mélisande . . . Je suis tout près de toi; je pleure de joie et cependant . . .

(He kisses her again.)

You're strange when I kiss you like that . . . You're so beautiful you'd think you were going to die . . .

Tu es étrange quand je t'embrasse ainsi . . . Tu es si belle qu'on dirait que tu vas mourir . . .

MELISANDE

So are you too . . .

Toi aussi . . .

PELLEAS

There, there . . . We cannot do what we want . . . I did not love you the first time I saw you . . .

Voilà, voilà . . . Nous ne faisons pas ce que nous voulons . . . Je ne t'aimais pas la première fois que je t'ai vue . . .

MELISANDE

Nor did I . . . I was afraid . . .

Moi non plus . . . J'avais peur . . .

PELLEAS

I could not look in your eyes . . . I wanted to go away at once . . . and then . . .

Je ne pouvais pas regarder tes yeux . . . Je voulais m'en aller tout de suite . . . et puis . . .

MELISANDE

I didn't want to come . . . I still don't know why I was afraid to come . . .

Moi, je ne voulais pas venir . . . Je ne sais pas encore pourquoi j'avais peur de venir . . .

PELLEAS

There are so many things we never know . . . We keep waiting . . . and then . . .] What is that noise? They're closing the gates! . . .

Il y a tant de choses qu'on ne saura jamais . . . Nous attendons toujours; et puis . . .] Quel est ce bruit? – On ferme les portes! . . .

MELISANDE

Yes, the gates are closed now . . .

Oui, on a fermé les portes . . .

So we cannot get back in. Do you hear the bolts? Listen! Those were the chains! Now it's too late, now it's too late!

Nous ne pouvons plus rentrer! – Entends-tu les verrous! – Écoute! écoute! . . . les grandes chaînes! . . . Il est trop tard, il est trop tard! . . .

MELISANDE

Oh good! That's good!

Tant mieux! tant mieux! [tant mieux!]

PELLEAS

You? You see, you see: It's no longer within our power! All is lost! All is won! All has been won tonight! Come! Come! My heart is beating so, it leaps to my throat . . .

Tu? . . . Voilà, voilà, . . . Ce n'est plus nous qui le voulons! . . . Tout est perdu, tout est sauvé! tout est sauvé ce soir! – Viens! viens . . . Mon cœur bat comme un fou jusqu'au fond de ma gorge . . .

(He takes her in his arms.) [37]

Listen! I feel my heart is nearly strangling me . . . Come! See the beauty of the shadows! . . .

Ecoute! écoute! mon cœur est sur le point de m'étrangler . . . Viens! Viens! . . . Ah! qu'il fait beau dans les ténèbres! . . .

MELISANDE

There is someone here, just behind us . . .

Il y a quelqu'un derrière nous! . . .

PELLEAS

I can't see anyone.

Je ne vois personne . . .

MELISANDE

I'm sure I heard a noise . . .

J'ai entendu du bruit . . .

PELLEAS

I hear only your heart beating in the darkness.

Je n'entends que ton cœur dans l'obscurité . . .

MELISANDE

I'm sure I heard the crackling of leaves . . .

J'ai entendu craquer les feuilles mortes . . .

PELLEAS

That's the wind growing suddenly still . . . The wind dropped while we kissed just now.

C'est le vent qui s'est tû tout à coup . . . Il est tombé pendant que nous nous embrassions . . .

MELISANDE

You see our shadows grow longer tonight . . .

Comme nos ombres sont grandes ce soir! . . .

PELLEAS

They intertwine and reach the end of the garden! Ah! Do you see them kissing over there? Look! Look!

Elles s'enlacent jusqu'au fond du jardin . . . Oh! qu'elles s'embrassent loin de nous! . . . Regarde! Regarde! . . .

MELISANDE
(in a stifled voice)

Ah! He's behind a tree!

A-a-h! – Il est derrière un arbre!

PELLEAS

Who?

Qui?

MELISANDE

Golaud!

Golaud!

PELLEAS

Golaud? Where? I see nothing.

Golaud? – où donc? – je ne vois rien . . .

MELISANDE

There . . . at the end of our shadows . . .

Là . . . au bout de nos ombres . . .

PELLEAS

Yes, yes; I can see him ... Don't turn away
too suddenly ...

Oui, oui; je l'ai vu ... Ne nous retournons
pas brusquement ...

MELISANDE

He's got his sword ...

Il a son épée ...

PELLEAS

I haven't got mine here ...

Je n'ai pas la mienne ...

MELISANDE

He saw, I know he saw us kissing ...

Il a vu que nous nous embrassions ...

PELLEAS

He doesn't know that we've seen him ...
Don't move an inch; don't turn your head
or he might rush out ... [He'll stay there so
long as he thinks we don't know.] He's
watching us ... He's standing there
without moving. You go, now go, go at
once, this way ... I'll wait for him ... I'll
keep him off ...

Il ne sait pas que nous l'avons vu ... Ne
bouge pas; ne tourne pas la tête ... Il se
précipiterait ... [Il restera là tant qu'il
croira que nous ne savons pas ...] Il nous
observe ... Il est encore immobile ... Va-
t'en, va-t'en tout de suite par ici ... Je
l'attendrai ... Je l'arrêterai ...

MELISANDE

No! No!

Non, non, non! ...

PELLEAS

Quickly! He saw it all! He'll kill us both!

Va-t'en! va-t'en! Il a tout vu! ... Il nous
tuera! ...

MELISANDE

Let him! Let him!

Tant mieux! tant mieux! tant mieux! ...

PELLEAS

Here he comes! Your lips! Your lips!

Il vient! il vient! ... Ta bouche! ... Ta
bouche! ...

MELISANDE

Yes! ... Yes! ... Yes!

Oui! ... oui! ... oui! ...

(They embrace passionately.)

PELLEAS

Oh! Oh! All the stars of heaven are falling!

Oh! oh! Toutes les étoiles tombent! ...

MELISANDE

On me as well! On me as well!

Sur moi aussi! sur moi aussi ...

PELLEAS

Again, yes, again! Be mine!

Encore! Encore! ... donne! donne! ...

MELISANDE

I'm all yours! all yours! all yours!

Toute! toute! toute!

*(Golaud falls upon them, sword in hand, and strikes down Pelléas who falls at the edge of the
well. Mélisande flies in terror.)*

MELISANDE
(in flight)

Oh, oh, I have no more courage!
I have no more courage! ... Ah!

Oh! oh! Je n'ai pas de courage!
... Je n'ai pas de courage! ...

(Golaud follows her through the woods in silence.)

84

Act Five

[¹**Scene One.** *A basement room in the castle. A group of servants is discovered, while children play outside one of the windows.*

OLD SERVANT

Wait and see, wait and see, girls; it's this evening. They'll tell us presently . . .

Vous verrez, vous verrez, mes filles; ce sera pour ce soir. – On viendra nous avertir tout à l'heure . . .

ANOTHER SERVANT

They won't tell us . . . They don't know what they're doing any more . . .

On ne viendra pas nous avertir . . . Ils ne savent plus ce qu'ils font . . .

SERVANT 3

Let's wait here . . .

Attendons ici . . .

SERVANT 4

We'll know when we have to go up . . .

Nous saurons bien quand il faudra monter . . .

SERVANT 5

When the time comes we'll go of our own accord . . .

Quand le moment sera venu, nous monterons de nous-mêmes . . .

SERVANT 6

There's no sound in the castle . . .

On n'entend plus aucun bruit dans la maison . . .

SERVANT 7

The children playing by the windows there should be told to be quiet.

Il faudrait faire taire les enfants qui jouent devant le soupirail.

SERVANT 8

They'll be quiet all on their own soon.

Ils se tairont d'eux-mêmes tout à l'heure.

SERVANT 9

It's not time yet . . .

Le moment n'est pas encore venu . . .

(An old servant comes in.)

OLD SERVANT

No one else is to go into the chamber. I've been listening for over an hour . . .
You could hear the flies crawling up the doors . . . I didn't hear a sound . . .

Personne ne peut plus entrer dans la chambre. J'ai écouté plus d'une heure . . . On entendrait marcher les mouches sur les portes . . . Je n'ai rien entendu . . .

SERVANT 1

Has she been left all alone in her chamber?

Est-ce qu'on l'a laissée seule dans sa chambre?

OLD SERVANT

No, no. I think it's full of people.

Non, non; je crois que la chambre est pleine de monde.

SERVANT 1

They'll be coming, they'll be coming soon . . .

On viendra, on viendra, tout à l'heure . . .

---

¹ This whole scene is omitted from the opera.

OLD SERVANT

My God! My God! No happiness comes into this house . . . One can't speak, but if I could tell what I know . . .

Mon Dieu! Mon Dieu! Ce n'est pas le bonheur qui est entré dans la maison . . . On ne peut pas parler, mais si je pouvais dire ce que je sais . . .

SERVANT 2

Was it you that found them by the gate?

C'est vous qui les avez trouvés devant la porte?

OLD SERVANT

Yes it was. It was me who found them. The porter says he saw them first, but it was me who woke him. He was lying asleep on his stomach and wouldn't get up. And now he says 'I saw them first'. Is that fair? Look here, I burnt myself lighting a lamp to go down to the cellar. What was I going down to the cellar for? I can't remember. So, I get up at five; it was still quite dark. I say to myself, I'll go across the courtyard and open the gate. Right. So I go down the stairs on tiptoe and open the gate as if it were a normal door . . . My God! My God! What do I see? Guess what I saw?

Mais oui, mais oui; c'est moi qui les ai trouvés. Le portier dit que c'est lui qui les a vus le premier; mais c'est moi qui l'ai réveillé. Il dormait sur le ventre et ne voulait pas se lever. – Et maintenant il vient dire: C'est moi qui les ai vus le premier. Est-ce que c'est juste? – Voyez-vous, je m'étais brûlée en allumant une lampe pour descendre à la cave. – Qu'est-ce que j'allais donc faire à la cave? – Je ne peux plus me rappeler. – Enfin je me lève à cinq heures; il ne faisait pas encore très clair; je me dis, je vais traverser la cour, et puis, je vais ouvrir la porte. Bien; je descends l'escalier sur la pointe des pieds et j'ouvre la porte comme si c'était une porte ordinaire . . . Mon Dieu! Mon Dieu! Qu'est-ce que je vois! Devinez un peu ce que je vois! . . .

SERVANT 1

They were outside the gate?

Ils étaient devant la porte?

OLD SERVANT

They were both stretched out outside the gate! Just like starving beggars . . . They were clutching each other like frightened children . . . The little princess was nearly dead, and big Golaud still had his sword sticking in his side . . . There was blood on the gateway . . .

Ils étaient étendus tous les deux devant la porte! . . . Tout à fait comme des pauvres qui ont faim . . . Ils étaient serrés l'un contre l'autre comme des petits enfants qui ont peur . . . La petite princesse était presque morte, et le grand Golaud avait encore son épée dans le côté . . . Il y avait du sang sur le seuil . . . .

SERVANT 2

Tell the children to be quiet . . . They're yelling out there by the window . . .

Il faudrait faire taire les enfants . . . Ils crient de toutes leurs forces devant le soupirail . . .

SERVANT 3

We can't hear what's being said . . .

On n'entend plus ce qu'on dit . . .

SERVANT 4

There's no point; I've already tried. They don't want to be quiet . . .

Il n'y a rien à faire; j'ai déjà essayé, ils ne veulent pas se taire . . .

SERVANT 1

He's almost recovered, hasn't he?

Il paraît qu'il est presque guéri?

OLD SERVANT

Who?

Qui?

SERVANT 1

Big Golaud.

Le grand Golaud.

SERVANT 3

Yes, yes. They took him to his wife's chamber. I met them just now in the passage. They were supporting him as if he was drunk. He can't yet walk on his own.

Oui, oui; on l'a conduit dans la chambre de sa femme. Je les ai rencontrés tout à l'heure, dans le corridor. On le soutenait comme s'il était ivre. Il ne peut pas encore marcher seul.

OLD SERVANT

He couldn't kill himself; he's too big. But she's scarcely hurt at all and she it is who's going to die . . . What do you make of that?

Il n'a pas pu se tuer; il est trop grand. Mais elle n'est presque pas blessée et c'est elle qui va mourir . . . Comprenez-vous cela?

SERVANT 1

Did you see the wound?

Vous avez vu la blessure?

OLD SERVANT

As clearly as I see you, my girl. I saw everything, you understand. I saw it before anyone else. A tiny wound below her left breast. A little wound that wouldn't kill a pigeon. Is that natural?

Comme je vous vois, ma fille. – J'ai tout vu, vous comprenez . . . Je l'ai vue avant tous les autres . . . Une toute petite blessure sous son petit sein gauche. Une petite blessure qui ne ferait pas mourir un pigeon. Est-ce que c'est naturel?

SERVANT 1

Yes, yes. There's something behind all this . . .

Oui, oui; il y a quelque chose là-dessous . . .

SERVANT 2

Yes, but she was delivered three days ago . . .

Oui, mais elle est accouchée il y a trois jours . . .

OLD SERVANT

Precisely! She was delivered on her death bed. Isn't that an obvious sign? And the child! Have you seen it? A little tiny girl a beggar wouldn't want to bring into the world . . . A little wax figure come much too soon . . . A little wax figure that has to live in lamb's wool . . . yes, yes, no happiness comes to this house . . .

Justement! . . . Elle a accouché sur son lit de mort; est-ce que ce n'est pas un grand signe? – Et quel enfant! L'avez-vous vu? – Une toute petite fille qu'un pauvre ne voudrait pas mettre au monde . . . Une petite figure de cire qui est venue beaucoup trop tôt . . . une petite figure de cire qui doit vivre dans de la laine d'agneau . . . oui, oui; ce n'est pas le bonheur qui est entré dans la maison . . .

SERVANT 1

Yes, yes, it's the hand of God at work.

Oui, oui; c'est la main de Dieu qui a remué . . .

SERVANT 3

Then there's the noble lord Pelléas . . . Where is he? No one knows.

C'est comme le bon seigneur Pelléas . . . où est-il? – Personne ne le sait . . .

OLD SERVANT

Yes they do, everyone knows. But no one dares say . . . We don't talk about this, we don't talk about that. We don't talk about anything. We don't tell the truth any more. But I do know he was found at the bottom of the Blind Man's Well. But no one, no one has been able to see him. There we are. Only at the final day will we know all this . . .

Si, si; tout le monde le sait . . . Mais personne n'ose en parler . . . On ne parle pas de ceci . . . on ne parle pas de cela . . . on ne parle plus de rien . . . on ne dit plus la vérité . . . Mais moi, je sais qu'on l'a trouvé au fond de la fontaine des aveugles . . . mais personne, personne n'a pu le voir . . . Voilà, voilà, on ne saura tout cela qu'au dernier jour . . .

SERVANT 1

I daren't sleep here any more . . .

Je n'ose plus dormir ici . . .

OLD SERVANT

When misfortune has entered the house, there's little cause to be silent . . .	Quand le malheur est dans la maison, on a beau se taire . . .

SERVANT 3

It finds you out all the same . . .	Il vous trouve tout de même . . .

SERVANT 1

They're afraid of us now . . .	Ils ont peur de nous maintenant . . .

SERVANT 2

They're all silent . . .	Ils se taisent tous . . .

SERVANT 3

They lower their eyes in the passages.	Ils baissent les yeux dans les corridors.

SERVANT 4

They only ever whisper.	Ils ne parlent plus qu'à voix basse.

SERVANT 5

You'd think they'd all done it together . . .	On dirait qu'ils l'ont fait tous ensemble . . .

SERVANT 6

There's no knowing what they've done . . .	On ne sait pas ce qu'ils ont fait . . .

SERVANT 7

What's to be done when the masters are afraid?	Que faut-il faire quand les maîtres ont peur? . . .

(*silence*)

SERVANT 1

I can't hear the children any more.	Je n'entends plus crier les enfants.

SERVANT 2

They've sat down by the window.	Ils se sont assis devant le soupirail.

SERVANT 3

They're huddling together.	Ils sont serrés les uns contre les autres.

OLD SERVANT

I can't hear any sound in the house.	Je n'entends plus rien dans la maison . . .

SERVANT 1

I can't even hear the children breathing . . .	On n'entend plus même respirer les enfants . . .

OLD SERVANT

Come along, come along. It's time to go up.	Venez, venez; il est temps de monter . . .

(*They all go out in silence.*)]

[1]**Scene Two.** *A room in the castle. Arkel, Golaud, and the Doctor are discovered in a corner of the room; Mélisande is lying on the bed.* [38]

DOCTOR

It would not be from such a little wound as this that she might die. It's not grave enough to kill a bird . . . So it is not you that killed her, my noble lord. Do not distress yourself so much. [She could not live . . . She was born for no reason . . . just to die . . .] And then no one has said yet that we will not save her . . .	Ce n'est pas de cette petite blessure qu'elle peut mourir; un oiseau n'en serait pas mort . . . ce n'est donc pas vous qui l'avez tuée, mon bon seigneur; ne vous désolez pas ainsi . . . [Elle ne pouvait pas vivre . . . Elle est née sans raison . . . pour mourir; et elle meurt sans raison . . .] Et puis, il n'est pas dit que nous ne la sauverons pas . . .

---

[1] Scene One of the opera.

ARKEL

No, no, I feel that in this chamber we are unnecessarily silent ... it is not a good sign ... See how she sleeps ... in a daze ... in a daze ... One would think that all life had gone out of her soul ...

Non, non; il me semble que nous nous taisons trop, malgré nous, dans sa chambre ... Ce n'est pas un bon signe ... Regardez comme elle dort ... lentement, lentement ... on dirait que son âme a froid pour toujours ...

GOLAUD

I have killed without cause! Is that not pain enough to make stones break out weeping? They were kissing like children, just playing games ... They were brother and sister ... And then, then on an impulse ... But I did it without meaning to, without meaning to ...

J'ai tué sans raison! Est-ce que ce n'est pas à faire pleurer les pierres! Ils s'étaient embrassés comme des petits enfants ... Ils s'étaient simplement embrassés. Ils étaient frère et sœur ... et moi, moi tout de suite! ... Je l'ai fait malgré moi, voyez-vous ... Je l'ai fait malgré moi ...

DOCTOR

One moment; she seems to be waking ...

Attention; je crois qu'elle s'éveille ...

MELISANDE

Open the window ... open the window ... [39]

Ouvrez la fenêtre ... ouvrez la fenêtre ...

ARKEL

Shall I open this one, Mélisande?

Veux-tu que j'ouvre celle-ci, Mélisande?

MELISANDE

No, no, open the big one ... so that I can see ...

Non, non; la grande fenêtre ... c'est pour voir ...

ARKEL

Don't you find the sea air too cold tonight?

Est-ce que l'air de la mer n'est pas trop froid ce soir?

DOCTOR

Open it; open it ...

Faites, faites ...

MELISANDE

Thank you ... Tell me, is that the sunset?

Merci ... Est-ce le soleil qui se couche?

ARKEL

Yes, that is the sun setting over the sea. It is late. How are you feeling, Mélisande?

Oui; c'est le soleil qui se couche sur la mer; il est tard. – Comment te trouves-tu, Mélisande?

MELISANDE

Well, – well. Why do you ask me that? I have never felt better ... And yet I feel there is something I know ...

Bien, bien. – Pourquoi demandez-vous cela? je n'ai jamais été mieux portante. – Il me semble cependant que je sais quelque chose ...

ARKEL

What do you mean? I don't understand.

Que dis-tu? – Je ne te comprends pas ...

MELISANDE

Neither do I understand what I'm saying, do you see? I don't know what I'm saying. I don't know what I know ... I can no longer say what I mean ...

Je ne comprends pas non plus tout ce que je dis, voyez-vous ... Je ne sais pas ce que je dis ... Je ne sais pas ce que je sais ... Je ne dis plus ce que je veux ...

ARKEL

But yes, you can ... It gladdens my heart to hear you speak like that; your mind has been wandering these few days so we could not understand you ... But now, those days are past and gone ...

Mais si, mais si ... Je suis tout heureux de t'entendre parler ainsi; tu as eu un peu de délire ces jours-ci, et l'on ne te comprenait plus ... Mais maintenant, tout cela est bien loin ...

I do not know . . . Grandfather, are you alone here in this chamber?	Je ne sais pas . . . – Etes-vous tout seul dans la chambre, grand-père?

No, the doctor who tended you is here too.	Non; il y a encore le médecin qui t'a guérie . . .

Ah!	Ah . . .

Also there is someone else . . .	Et puis il y a encore quelqu'un . . .

Who is it?	Qui est-ce?

It's . . . but I must not frighten you. He wishes you no harm, I assure you. If you're afraid, he'll go away. He is a most unhappy man . . .	C'est . . . il ne faut pas t'effrayer . . . Il ne te veut pas le moindre mal, sois-en sûre . . . Si tu as peur, il s'en ira . . . Il est très malheureux . . .

Who is it?	Qui est-ce?

It's . . . it's your husband, it's Golaud . . .	C'est . . . c'est ton mari . . . c'est Golaud . . .

Golaud is here? Why doesn't he come near me?	Golaud est ici? Pourquoi ne vient-il pas près de moi?

(dragging himself to the bed)

Mélisande . . . Mélisande . . .	Mélisande . . . Mélisande . . .

Is that you, Golaud? I can scarcely recognise you. The evening sun is shining in my eyes . . . Why are you looking at the walls? You look thinner and older. Has it been a long time since we last saw each other?	Est-ce vous, Golaud? Je ne vous reconnaissais presque plus . . . C'est que j'ai le soleil du soir dans les yeux . . . Pourquoi regardez-vous les murs? Vous avez maigri et vieilli . . . Y a-t-il longtemps que nous ne nous sommes vus?

(to Arkel and the Doctor)

Would you kindly leave us now for a while, my poor friends . . . But I will leave the chamber door wide open . . . Only for a moment . . . I have something that I wish to say to her; otherwise I could not die in peace. Will you go? [Go to the end of the passage.] You may come back again in a moment. Do not refuse me this request. You see my misfortune.	Voulez-vous vous éloigner un instant, mes pauvres amis . . . Je laisserai la porte grande ouverte . . . Un instant seulement . . . Je voudrais lui dire quelque chose; sans cela je ne pourrais pas mourir . . . Voulez-vous? –[Allez jusqu'au bout du corridor;] vous pouvez revenir tout de suite . . . Ne me refusez pas cela . . . Je suis un malheureux . . .

(Arkel and the Doctor go out.)

Mélisande, do you pity me, as I pity you? Mélisande? Do you forgive me, Mélisande?	Mélisande, as-tu pitié de moi, comme j'ai pitié de toi? . . . Mélisande? . . . Me pardonnes-tu, Mélisande? . . .

Yes, yes, I forgive you . . . What is there to[40] forgive?	Oui, oui, je te pardonne . . . Que faut-il pardonner?

I've wronged you so, Mélisande . . . I cannot tell you what wrong I have done . . .	Je t'ai fait tant de mal, Mélisande . . . Je ne puis pas te dire le mal que je t'ai fait . . .

But today I can see it all so clearly ... From the very first day ... [Everything I have not known before is obvious to me this evening.] And it is all my fault, everything that has happened. Everything that will happen too. Oh, if I could only tell you, you would see how I see it now ... I see it all, I see it all! But I loved you so! I loved you so! But now someone will die ... It is I that will die ... And I would like to know ... I would like to ask you ... You will not mind my asking? [I would like ...] One must always tell the truth to someone who's going to die ... In his last hour he must know the truth, otherwise he could never sleep in peace. Will you swear to tell me the truth?

Mais je le vois, je le vois si clairement aujourd'hui ... depuis le premier jour ... [Et tout ce que je ne savais pas jusqu'ici, me saute aux yeux ce soir ...] Et tout est de ma faute, tout ce qui est arrivé, tout ce qui va arriver ... Si je pouvais le dire, tu verrais comme je le vois! ... Je vois tout, je vois tout! ... Mais je t'aimais tant! ... Je t'aimais tant! ... Mais maintenant, quelqu'un va mourir ... C'est moi qui vais mourir ... Et je voudrais savoir ... Je voudrais te demander ... Tu ne m'en voudras pas? ... [Je voudrais ...] Il faut dire la vérité à quelqu'un qui va mourir ... Il faut qu'il sache la vérité, sans cela il ne pourrait pas dormir ... Me jures-tu de dire la vérité?

MELISANDE

Yes.

Oui.

GOLAUD

Did you love Pelléas?

As-tu aimé Pelléas?

MELISANDE

Why yes; yes, I loved him. Where is he?

Mais oui; je l'ai aimé. Où est-il?

GOLAUD

Do you not understand me? Don't you want to understand me? I feel ... What I feel is ... It's this, tell me this: I ask you whether you loved him with a forbidden love. Did you? Tell me, were you guilty? Tell me, tell me! Yes, yes, yes?

Tu ne me comprends pas? – Tu ne veux pas me comprendre? – Il me semble ... Il me semble ... Eh bien, voici: Je te demande si tu l'as aimé d'un amour défendu? ... As-tu ... avez-vous été coupables? Dis, dis, oui, oui, oui? ...

MELISANDE

No, no, no, we were not guilty ... Why do you ask me that?

Non, non; nous n'avons pas été coupables. – Pourquoi demandez-vous cela?

GOLAUD

Mélisande! Tell me the truth, for the love of God!

Mélisande! ... dis-moi la vérité pour l'amour de Dieu!

MELISANDE

Why? Wasn't that the truth I told you?

Pourquoi n'ai-je pas dit la vérité?

GOLAUD

Do not go on lying at the moment of death!

Ne mens plus ainsi, au moment de mourir!

MELISANDE

Who is going to die? Is it me?

Qui est-ce qui va mourir? – Est-ce moi?

GOLAUD

You, you, and me, me as well, after you! And we need the truth, we now need the truth! Do you hear? Tell me all, tell me everything! I forgive you everything!

Toi, toi! et moi, moi aussi, après toi! ... Et il nous faut la vérité ... Il nous faut enfin la vérité, entends-tu! ... Dis-moi tout! Dis-moi tout! Je te pardonne tout! ...

MELISANDE

Why am I going to die? I did not know ...

Pourquoi vais-je mourir? – Je ne le savais pas ...

GOLAUD

But you now understand, now you know ... Quickly! Quickly! Tell me the truth! Tell me the truth!

Tu le sais maintenant! ... Il est temps! Il est temps! ... Vite! vite! ... La vérité! la vérité! ...

The truth . . . the truth . . . the truth . . .   La vérité . . . la vérité . . .

GOLAUD

Where are you, Mélisande! Where are you?   Où es-tu? – Mélisande! – Où es-tu? Ce
It's not natural. Mélisande! Where are   n'est pas naturel! Mélisande! Où es-tu? Où
you?   vas-tu?

(catching sight of Arkel and the Doctor at the door)

Yes, yes, you may come in . . . I know   Oui, oui; vous pouvez rentrer . . . Je ne sais
nothing, it's useless, [it's too late,] she is   rien; c'est inutile . . . [Il est trop tard;] elle
already too far from us . . . I shall never   est déjà trop loin de nous . . . Je ne saurai
know. I shall die here like a blind man . . .   jamais! . . . Je vais mourir ici comme un
          aveugle! . . .

ARKEL

What have you done? You will kill her,   Qu'avez-vous fait? Vous allez la tuer . . .
Golaud . . .

GOLAUD

I have killed her already . . .   Je l'ai déjà tuée . . .

ARKEL

Mélisande . . .   Mélisande . . .

MELISANDE

Is that you, Grandfather?   Est-ce vous, grand-père?

ARKEL

Yes, my daughter; tell me, what can I do?   Oui, ma fille . . . Que veux-tu que je fasse?

MELISANDE

Is it true that the winter's coming?   Est-il vrai que l'hiver commence?

ARKEL

Why do you ask a thing like that?   Pourquoi demandes-tu cela?

MELISANDE

Because it's cold now, and there are no   Parce qu'il fait froid et qu'il n'y a plus de
leaves left . . .   feuilles . . .

ARKEL

Are you cold? Would you like the windows   Tu as froid? – Veux-tu qu'on ferme les
shut?   fenêtres?

MELISANDE

No . . . Do not close them till the sun has set   Non, non . . . jusqu'à ce que le soleil soit au
under the sea. Since it's setting so slowly   fond de la mer. – Il descend lentement,
the winter must already be with us.   alors c'est l'hiver qui commence?

ARKEL

[Yes.] Do you not like the winter?   [Oui. –] Tu n'aimes pas l'hiver?

MELISANDE

Oh, no! I'm frightened of the cold, I'm so   Oh! non. J'ai peur du froid – Ah! J'ai peur
frightened of cold . . .   des grands froids . . .

ARKEL

Are you better now?   Te sens-tu mieux?

MELISANDE

Yes, yes, All the worries that I had are   Oui, oui; je n'ai plus toutes ces inquiét-
gone . . .   udes . . .

ARKEL

Would you like to see your child?   Veux-tu voir ton enfant?

MELISANDE

What child?   Quel enfant?

Your own child. Your little daughter. [You have brought a little girl into the world.]

Ton enfant. – [1]Tu es mère . . . [Tu as mis au monde une petite fille . . .]

MELISANDE

Where is she?

Où est-elle?

ARKEL

She's here.

Ici . . .

MELISANDE

How strange . . . I cannot lift my arms to take her . . .

C'est étrange . . . je ne puis pas lever les bras pour la prendre . . .

ARKEL

That is because you are so weak still. I will hold her myself; look at her . . .

C'est que tu es encore très faible . . . Je la tiendrai moi-même; regarde . . .

MELISANDE

But she does not smile . . . She is so tiny . . . She is going to cry, as well . . . I'm sorry for her . . .

Elle ne rit pas . . . Elle est petite . . . Elle va pleurer aussi . . . J'ai pitié d'elle . . .

(The chamber is gradually filled with the castle serving women, who line the walls and wait in silence.)

GOLAUD
(rising suddenly)

What is this? What are all these women doing here?

Qu'y a-t-il? – Qu'est-ce que toutes ces femmes viennent faire ici?

DOCTOR

They are the servants . . .

Ce sont les servantes . . .

ARKEL

Who sent for them to be here?

Qui est-ce qui les a appelées?

DOCTOR

Not I . . .

Ce n'est pas moi . . .

GOLAUD

What are you doing here? Did anybody summon you here? What have you come here for? What is all this about? Answer me!

Pourquoi venez-vous ici? – Personne ne vous a demandées . . . Que venez-vous faire ici? – Mais qu'est-ce que c'est donc? – Répondez! . . .

(The servants make no reply.)

ARKEL

You must not speak so loudly . . . She is going to sleep. She has closed her eyes . . .

Ne parlez pas trop fort . . . Elle va dormir; elle a fermé les yeux . . .

GOLAUD

Do you think? . . .

Ce n'est pas? . . .

DOCTOR

No, no. Look, she is breathing . . .

Non, non; voyez, elle respire . . .

ARKEL

Her eyes are full of tears. But in truth it's her soul that is weeping . . . Why is she stretching out her arms? What does she want?

Ses yeux sont pleins de larmes. – Maintenant c'est son âme qui pleure . . . Pourquoi étend-elle ainsi les bras? – Que veut-elle?

DOCTOR

Clearly she wants her child. That's a desperate mother's struggle . . .

C'est vers l'enfant sans doute. C'est la lutte de la mère contre la mort . . .

---

[1] Ta petite fille . . .

GOLAUD

What do you mean? Has it come to that? You must tell me, tell me! Tell me!

En ce moment? – En ce moment? – Il faut le dire, dites! dites!

DOCTOR

It could be . . .

Peut-être . . .

GOLAUD

Any moment? Oh! Oh! I must tell her . . . Mélisande! Mélisande! Leave me alone! Leave me alone with her!

Tout de suite? . . . Oh! Oh! Il faut que je lui dise . . . – Mélisande! Mélisande! . . . Laissez-moi seul! laissez-moi seul avec elle! . . .

ARKEL

No, no. Stand away. Don't trouble her now. Do not speak to her. You can never know how deeply the soul feels . . .

Non; non; n'approchez pas . . . Ne la troublez pas . . . Ne lui parlez plus . . . Vous ne savez pas ce que c'est que l'âme . . .

GOLAUD

I cannot be guilty! I cannot be guilty!

Ce n'est pas ma faute . . . Ce n'est pas ma faute!

ARKEL

Quiet! Quiet! Have a care . . . We must not speak too loudly at such a moment . . . She must not be disturbed, for the soul is a lover of silence . . . and should pass on alone to the next world. See how quietly she bears her pain. But the sadness, Golaud . . . But the sadness of everything we've seen . . . Oh! Oh!

Attention . . . Attention . . . Il faut parler à voix basse, maintenant – Il ne faut plus l'inquiéter . . . L'âme humaine est très silencieuse . . . L'âme humaine aime à s'en aller seule . . . Elle souffre si timidement . . . Mais la tristesse, Golaud . . . mais la tristesse de tout ce que l'on voit! . . . Oh! oh! oh! . . .

(At this moment all the servants fall on their knees at the back of the room.)

ARKEL
(turning)

What is it?

Qu'y a-t-il?

DOCTOR
(approaching the bed and touching the body)

They are right . . .

Elles ont raison . . .

[*(a long silence)*]

ARKEL

I saw nothing. Are you sure?

Je n'ai rien vu. – Etes-vous sûr? . . .

DOCTOR

Yes, yes.

Oui, oui.

ARKEL

I heard no sound . . . So quickly, so quickly . . . [Suddenly . . .] Gone without saying a word more . . .

Je n'ai rien entendu . . . Si vite, si vite . . . [Tout à coup . . .] Elle s'en va sans rien dire . . .

GOLAUD
(sobbing)

Oh! Oh!

Oh! oh! oh!

ARKEL

Don't linger here, Golaud . . . She needs to be left in silence. Come out now, come away . . . It is painful, but it is not your fault. She was such a quiet little creature, so shy and so silent . . . She was a poor little creature wrapped in mystery as we all are . . . There she lies as though she were the elder sister of her child . . . [Come now, come now . . . My God! My God! I shall

Ne restez pas ici, Golaud . . . Il lui faut le silence, maintenant . . . Venez, venez . . . C'est terrible, mais ce n'est pas votre faute . . . C'était un petit être si tranquille, si timide et si silencieux . . . C'était un pauvre petit être mystérieux, comme tout le monde . . . Elle est là, comme si elle était la grande soeur de son enfant . . . [Venez, venez . . . Mon Dieu! Mon Dieu! . . . Je n'y

never understand it . . . We must not stay here.] Come away! The child must not remain here in this chamber. Its life is precious, in place of its mother. Now it's the turn of her poor little daughter . . .

comprendrai rien non plus . . . non plus . . . Ne restons pas ici. –]Venez; il ne faut pas que l'enfant reste dans cette chambre . . . Il faut qu'il vive, maintenant, à sa place . . . C'est au tour de la pauvre petite . . .

(They go out in silence.)

Bibliography

Maurice Maeterlinck: A Study of his Life and Thought (Oxford, 1960) is a fascinating general study of the poet by W.D. Halls.

The fruit of a lifetime's work, Edward Lockspeiser's two volume *Debussy, his Life and Mind* (London 1962/5) is a very readable and sensitive introduction to the composer. It contains many quotations from Debussy's correspondence (otherwise unpublished in English) and sets the composer in the context of his period with fascinating cross-references to contemporary arts. Roger Nichols has written a short, more technical study of the composer's music (*Debussy*, Oxford 1973). Martin Cooper's *French Music from the Death of Berlioz to the Death of Fauré* (London, 1951) is a unique general survey of the music of the period.

Joseph Kerman's classically controversial *Opera as Drama* (New York, 1956) contains a chapter on the opera. Robin Holloway's *Debussy and Wagner* (Eulenberg, 1979) is an important and erudite analysis of *Pelléas* and *Tristan und Isolde*.

Three books now out of print which are still of interest are *La jeunesse de Pelléas: lettres de Claude Debussy à André Messager*, edited by J. André-Messager, (Paris, 1938); *Mary Garden's Story* (Mary Garden and Louis Biancolli, New York, 1951), containing the first Mélisande's reminiscences of her career; and Maurice Emmanuel's classic analysis of the opera: *Pelléas et Mélisande de Claude Debussy: étude historique et critique, analyse musicale* (Paris, 1925).

The score is published by United Music Publishers.

Discography Available recordings in stereo (unless asterisked *) and in French. Cassette tape numbers are also given. A valuable review by Felix Aprahamian of all performances on record is contained in *Opera on Record* (ed. Alan Blyth, Hutchinson 1979).

Conductor Company/Orchestra	*Ansermet* Suisse Romande	*Karajan* Deutsche Oper, Berlin	*Jordan* Monte Carlo Nat. Opera	*Boulez* Royal Opera, Covent Garden
Pelléas	Maurane	Stilwell	Tappy	Shirley
Mélisande	Spoorenberg	von Stade	Yakar	Söderström
Golaud	London	van Dam	Huttenlocher	McIntyre
Arkel	Hoekman	Raimondi	Loup	Ward
Geneviève	Veasey	Denize	Taillon	Minton
Yniold	Brédy	Barbaux	Alliot-Lugaz	Britten
Disc number UK	SET 277–9	SLS 5172	STU71296	77324
Tape number UK		TC–SLS 5172		
Disc number US	OSA 1379	SZX–3885		M3–30119

Excerpts

	Artists	Number
Excerpts	Nespoulos, Croiza, Maguenat, Dufranne, Narcon, *conductor* Truc.	GEMM 145 *
Excerpts	M. Teyte	GHP 4003 *

96